"This book provides effective tools for combating feelings of inadequacy, unworthiness, and low self-esteem that are so common among teens. Readers will learn strategies for self-acceptance, changing negative thinking patterns, and communicating effectively. The book is clear, easy to read, and filled with practical exercises. Highly recommended!"

—**Martin M. Antony, PhD, ABPP**, professor of psychology at Ryerson University in Toronto, ON, Canada, and coauthor of *The Shyness and Social Anxiety Workbook* and *The Anti-Anxiety Workbook*

"Just As You Are helps young people examine their negative self-stories from a place of compassion and value. The personal stories and exercises will resonate with a broad range of readers. Such a helpful book."

—**Ben Sedley, PhD**, clinical psychologist and author of *Stuff That Sucks*

"A beautiful guide to self-acceptance in the face of the relentless inner critic. The feeling that one isn't good enough, that one is unworthy, is a huge source of pain and paralysis. This book is a game changer, a healing breath of kindness and self-compassion."

—**Matthew McKay, PhD**, coauthor of *Self-Esteem*

"We all struggle with parts of ourselves and feel at some level *not* okay. But this common need to appear like you have it all together is not only exhausting and disconfirming, it's lonely as well. As you read others' stories of this same struggle, work through exercises, and challenge your inner critic, you learn to accept yourself *Just As You Are* with the same care and warmth that you would your best friend."

—**Janetti Marotta, PhD**, author of *50 Mindful Steps to Self-Esteem*

"So many young people struggle with feeling 'not good enough,' or believing that something is fundamentally wrong with them. *Just As You Are* is a step-by-step guide to undo those negative core beliefs. Michelle and Kelly Skeen offer tools for understanding yourself, identifying strengths, and changing unhealthy habits. They teach mindfulness and self-compassion in down-to-earth language that will appeal to everyone, even those who are skeptical of self-help books."

—**Ann Marie Dobosz, MA, MFT**, author of *The Perfectionism Workbook for Teens*

"Michelle Skeen has written yet another elegant, reassuring, and, most importantly, useful book. As with her other books, her hand reaches out from the pages with a powerful yet gentle message of guidance and encouragement. At a time when young people are feeling estranged, isolated, and not heard, Michelle offers her unique and reassuring voice; a lifeline from that dark place of self-aversion and unrelenting self-criticism to which many young people wake up each morning.

An addition to Michelle's wise counsel is the voice from her daughter Kelly. Too often young folks feel talked to and left not knowing where to begin in their journey of healing. Kelly, from her youthful wisdom, beautifully offers a 'Hey! Here's how this all works! See, it's not so hard!' What powerful encouragement!"

—**Thomas Roberts, LCSW**, psychotherapist, clinical hypnotherapist, mindfulness and meditation teacher and retreat leader, and author of *The Mindfulness Workbook*

"Michelle and Kelly Skeen have written a powerful tool to help teens navigate the tricky world of self-acceptance. Their words are thought-provoking, genuine, and kind. Teens will relate to the heartfelt stories and learn to embrace and appreciate their authentic self."

> —**Julia V. Taylor, PhD**, counselor educator at the University of Virginia in Charlottesville, VA; author of *The Body Image Workbook for Teens*; and coauthor of *The Bullying Workbook for Teens*

"*Just As You Are* speaks in a caring and thoughtful voice to the many teens who feel uncomfortable in their own skins. It's filled with carefully crafted exercises that rest on a foundation of self-acceptance and self-compassion. Teens will experience the power that comes with truly being themselves."

> —**Michael A. Tompkins, PhD, ABPP**, coauthor of *The Relaxation and Stress Reduction Workbook for Teens*, and codirector of the San Francisco Bay Area Center for Cognitive Therapy

the *i*nstant help solutions series

Young people today need mental health resources more than ever. That's why New Harbinger created the **Instant Help Solutions Series** especially for teens. Written by leading psychologists, physicians, and professionals, these evidence-based self-help books offer practical tips and strategies for dealing with a variety of mental health issues and life challenges teens face, such as depression, anxiety, bullying, eating disorders, trauma, and self-esteem problems.

Studies have shown that young people who learn healthy coping skills early on are better able to navigate problems later in life. Engaging and easy-to-use, these books provide teens with the tools they need to thrive—at home, at school, and on into adulthood.

This series is part of the **New Harbinger Instant Help Books** imprint, founded by renowned child psychologist Lawrence Shapiro. For a complete list of books in this series, visit newharbinger.com.

just as you are

a teen's guide to self-acceptance & lasting self-esteem

MICHELLE SKEEN, PsyD
KELLY SKEEN

Instant Help Books
An Imprint of New Harbinger Publications, Inc.

Publisher's Note

This publication is designed to provide accurate and authoritative information in regard to the subject matter covered. It is sold with the understanding that the publisher is not engaged in rendering psychological, financial, legal, or other professional services. If expert assistance or counseling is needed, the services of a competent professional should be sought.

Copyright © 2018 by Michelle Skeen and Kelly Skeen
Instant Help Books
An imprint of New Harbinger Publications, Inc.
5674 Shattuck Avenue
Oakland, CA 94609
www.newharbinger.com

Cover design by Amy Shoup; Acquired by Elizabeth Hollis Hansen; Edited by Kristi Hein

Library of Congress Cataloging-in-Publication Data

Names: Skeen, Michelle, author. | Skeen, Kelly, author.
Title: Just as you are : a teen's guide to self-acceptance and lasting self-esteem / Michelle Skeen and Kelly Skeen.
Identifiers: LCCN 2018022843 (print) | LCCN 2018026924 (ebook) | ISBN 9781626255913 (PDF e-book) | ISBN 9781626255920 (ePub) | ISBN 9781626255906 (pbk. : alk. paper)
Subjects: LCSH: Self-esteem in adolescence--Juvenile literature. | Self-acceptance--Juvenile literature. | Teenagers--Conduct of life--Juvenile literature.
Classification: LCC BF724.3.S36 (ebook) | LCC BF724.3.S36 S54 2018 (print) | DDC 155.5/182--dc23
LC record available at https://lccn.loc.gov/2018022843

Printed in the United States of America

24   23   22

15   14   13   12   11   10

To all teens who have ever felt different,
inadequate, unworthy, defective, or flawed

Contents

Acknowledgments

This book would not have been possible without the support of Matt McKay, Catharine Meyers, and Elizabeth Hollis Hansen. They supported our book from the beginning, understanding the importance of getting at the seedlings of negative beliefs before they take root as deeply held core beliefs. We also want to thank the entire New Harbinger family for supporting this project. There are so many individuals who nurtured this book from beginning to end. It is quite remarkable what they accomplish while making it such a pleasant experience for us. Thank you!

I want to thank my daughter, Kelly, for agreeing to write this book with me. When we wrote our first book, *Communication Skills for Teens*, we started it while she was in high school and finished it during her freshman year of college. As I write these words, she is almost halfway through her senior year in college. This writing project was a significant commitment given her demanding schedule at school (including writing a senior thesis that is the equivalent of a book). It is a uniquely wonderful experience to write a book together, and we have had the privilege of doing it twice. I have learned so much through this process, and I am forever grateful.

Big heart hugs to all of our friends who support us in big and little ways, and most importantly they accept us just as we are. C. S. Lewis said it best: "Friendship is born at that moment when one person says to another: What! You too? I thought I was the only one." It's nice to be reminded that we are never alone.

And, last but not least, to the three most important men in our lives—Jake, Eric (along with a big shout-out for your feedback on the manuscript), and Kelly's Daddio—you are simply the best!

Introduction

When you are feeling bad about yourself and struggling, you usually feel even worse because you feel alone with your pain. You might feel that if only someone understood your suffering it would make you feel better. But you also know that this would involve sharing the part or parts of yourself that you are trying to hide. If you feel inadequate, deficient, defective, flawed, or failing in some way, we want you to know that you are not alone. All of us struggle with some aspect of ourselves. This feeling is reinforced and likely made worse by social media and the constant and ever-changing messages you receive about what you need to do, to look like, and to act like in order to be accepted. It can leave you feeling like you need to hide parts of yourself that aren't perfect and/or don't fit within the current societal norm. This by itself feels like a setup for failure.

First, we want to explain a word that we use throughout the book—*defective*. This word represents a core belief that, we believe, everyone feels to some degree. It's a feeling that something is wrong with you. This feeling is on a spectrum—you may feel this a little bit, a decent amount, or a lot. You may feel it in some areas of your life and not others or all areas of your life. It may be something that is very specific to you or it might be related to your family or background or community. It might be something that you feel is obvious to everyone who sees you or it might be something that is not visibly obvious to others. Ultimately, the feeling is the same—there is something about yourself that causes you to feel shame.

When you feel like parts of yourself are unacceptable, then it's likely you feel shame. And the presence of shame is preventing you from being your authentic self and developing relationships that allow for a deep connection. It can feel impossible to share the parts of yourself that you have learned to hide, because you imagine or experience consequences if or when you share them. Everyone feels this way about some part of himself or herself. It may just be something that was passed down by your family—a type of survival mechanism—or it may be something you learned from peer interaction or societal expectations. Whatever the source, the result is the same: you are not fully living or enjoying your life.

Lifelong struggles with feelings of unworthiness and inferiority begin with beliefs formed in childhood and adolescence. This book empowers teens to identify and eliminate these beliefs now, before they take root and cause problems like depression, addiction, and failed relationships in adulthood. *Just As You Are* gives you a way to understand your feelings and change your perception of yourself as well as the influence of others.

First, you will look at the beliefs about yourself and others that are getting in the way of living the life you want and deserve. Understanding what started this cycle of negativity is the first step in eliminating it. You will learn how to liberate yourself from these feelings of defectiveness and distorted thoughts by accepting your imperfections and accepting your whole self. You will accomplish this by identifying your values—that is, deciding what's truly important to you. When you are solid in your values, you are less likely to feel overpowered by the opinions and criticisms of others.

You will then learn about compassion—most importantly, cultivating self-compassion, along with extending compassion to others, and being receptive to compassion from other people. Next, you will learn mindfulness as a tool for self-acceptance. When your self-defeating thoughts and beliefs are triggered, mindfulness can help you stay present with your current experience rather than reacting based on past failures.

With these skills, you will be prepared to understand your emotions, tolerate the discomfort they may bring, and take actions that will move you toward what's important to you. And you will learn effective communication skills so you can connect with other people in a meaningful way.

All of this will allow you to be authentic and accept yourself—just as you are—and create and maintain deep connections with others.

chapter 1

What's Up with the Way
I Feel about Myself?

Whether you are twelve years old or nineteen years old, your beliefs about yourself have already been formed by your interactions with your environment. Your environment includes everything you come in contact with—social media, family, friends, peers, your school, community, books you read, TV shows and movies you watch, magazines … you get the picture. And they all communicate or interact with you in a way that creates and reinforces your beliefs about yourself, others, and the world around you.

If these early beliefs lead you to feel that you are somehow not worthy, or inferior, they have the potential to become so established that they become difficult to eliminate. As you continue reading and complete the exercises in this book, you'll begin to understand and identify the negative beliefs about yourself, meet them with self-compassion, and accept yourself just as you are. The exercises in this book will help you gain insights into your experiences that can lead you to an adult-hood of greater ease, confidence, and resilience in the face of all of life's ups and downs.

As you might imagine, your beliefs about yourself are a mixed bag. It's likely that you have beliefs about yourself that are positive. Maybe you make friends easily, you have great hair, you are close with your siblings, you excel academically, you're good at sports, and so on. And it's also likely that you have beliefs about yourself that are negative. In fact, this might mean that you are hiding parts of yourself because you fear being judged, not accepted, or both. You may feel that you are outside of the "norm" in some way. There might even be aspects of your identity that you have no control over or you don't like—such as your ethnicity, religion, family, culture, height, eye color, body type ... you get the point. Of course, there is even more of your life that is out of your control, because you have parental figures who control parts of your life that you have little or no say about—where you live, what school you attend, activities you are or are not allowed to participate in, who you can be friends with, who you can date—the list goes on. And there's a good chance that you feel inadequate, flawed, or not good enough as a result of some of these factors.

This book is designed to help you bring awareness to the negative beliefs that might be getting in the way of pursuing your interests, taking chances, exploring and sharing all parts of yourself, and building meaningful relationships. This new awareness includes identifying and understanding the way that your current behaviors are likely reinforcing your negative beliefs about yourself. First, you will look at the beliefs about yourself and others that are getting in the way of accepting all parts of yourself. Understanding what started this cycle of negativity is the first step in eliminating it. After you've brought awareness to your beliefs, you will learn how to handle the negative thoughts that can feel like they reinforce your negative beliefs, and you'll get the tools you need to break free from the behaviors that reinforce these feelings of defectiveness, unworthiness, failure, and inadequacy.

Your Negative Beliefs

Every teenager (you are not alone!) struggles to some extent with feelings of inadequacy, defectiveness, and unworthiness. This impacts your feelings of self-worth, which might be holding you back or getting in the way of satisfying peer interactions and acceptance. Like most people, you care what other people think of you, and you probably spend at least some time comparing yourself to your peers. Social media feeds our natural tendency to see how we measure up to others. This can result in feeling that you are flawed—not as perfect as other people might seem. When these feelings get repeatedly reinforced over time, it can lead to shame, depression, anxiety, and isolation.

We are all wired to connect with others, and when we do make healthy connections, we thrive. So it makes sense that we would want to be accepted by others, and we would fear being found not good enough and rejected. In fact, you may go to great lengths to avoid judgment or rejection from others. This might include seeking affirmation from others, being unable or unwilling to make decisions without approval from others, or having difficulty hearing even mild criticism. You may find it difficult to accept and share parts of yourself that are out of your control, or you may feel like you need to be a certain way in order to be liked and accepted by others. Or you may focus more of your energy on others as a way to distract them from the ways in which you feel insufficient. You may already be thinking about the parts of yourself that make you feel less than, or that you hide from others because you fear the response you might receive. And you might even be aware of the ways this holds you back from realizing your full potential or building the relationships that you long for.

Let's hear stories from some teens who have shared their feelings of defectiveness and how it impacts their lives.

Kamele

Kamele is the center on his high school varsity basketball team. A silent warrior, he works hard and is popular and well-liked, but he's quiet. His friends and peers take his silence as a sign that he's just cool. After all, he doesn't need to say much; he's too busy winning basketball games and being a reliable teammate and friend.

Now let's hear from Kamele about his experience:

I'm terrified to say much to anyone because I'm afraid that they will think I'm stupid. When I was younger and we lived in a different city, I developed a stutter. My parents sent me to a speech therapist. I was able to get rid of it, for the most part, over time. But when I'm nervous or stressed it resurfaces. I remember the ridicule that I experienced when I was younger. It was so painful. There were days when I wouldn't get out of bed to go to school. Now I hide this part of myself because I am scared that I will be judged as inadequate and rejected.

Kamele's external presentation, as a high school basketball star, is a contrast to his internal experience. This often creates a barrier for him when trying to form deeper, more authentic connections with others. We fear rejection if others see the parts of us that we experience as imperfect, inadequate, defective, or flawed. Do you worry that others will view you unfavorably if they become aware of any areas where you struggle?

Gaia

Gaia is a social media star. She has thousands of Facebook "friends," and followers on Instagram and Snapchat. She is beautiful and clever. People can't help but "like" her posts. She wears the most trendy, sought-after clothes, often in interesting ways, and she always accompanies her posted photos with a clever caption. Everyone wants to either be her or be her friend.

Here is Gaia's experience:

Every moment of my day is preoccupied with thoughts about what I need to do to be liked. I plan out my posts on social media with excruciating detail. Most of the time I take at least twenty selfies before I pick one that's good enough to post. Then I edit it and choose a filter that makes me look the way I want to. Once I've done that, I agonize over creating a caption to post with the photo. It's like I live in constant fear that I won't be liked by my peers. I don't really have any truly close friends because I'm afraid to let them see that my "perfect posts" are very different from how imperfect I feel.

Gaia has carefully cultivated an image that she wants to project to others. Making constant comparisons on social media has decreased her feelings of self-worth because she feels like she needs to be viewed a particular way in order to be "liked"—whether on social media or in real life. The pressure of trying to maintain this false front compromises her ability to make authentic connections with others. Do you feel like you're invested in presenting yourself in a favorable light in order to be liked and to hide parts of yourself that you don't like?

Layla

Layla started seeing a psychiatrist and taking antidepressant medication when she was ten years old. As an only child, she spent lots of time alone. Her parents began to worry that something was wrong because she didn't show an interest in spending time with her peers or engaging in activities that seemed typical of kids her age. Once she started on the medication she became less isolated and seemed more interested in getting involved in activities with her peers.

Let's hear what Layla has to say about her experience:

I've been on antidepressant medication for four years. It really does feel like it's changed my life. And it's nice that my parents aren't worried about me all of the time. I have friends, and I stay busy with activities, but I feel a lot of shame about being a "crazy person" who needs to be on medication. None of my friends know that I take medication to help with my depression. In fact, I put on such a happy front that they sometimes call me the cheerleader. I worry that if they ever found out that I'm "crazy" they wouldn't want to be friends with me anymore.

Fortunately, Layla's parents and doctor were able to identify her depression and treat it with the proper medication so she can enjoy her life. Clearly, her condition is something that is out of her control, and yet she is hiding this part of herself and her experience because she fears that she will be rejected by her peers. Do you have a medical or other condition that you hide from others?

Jeff

Jeff is a good guy with a good family. He does well in school, and he is good at most sports. He makes friends easily, but he never feels like he's good enough. So he goes out of his way to please people. He tells others what they want to hear. This might include things about them, himself, or other topics. Jeff can be whoever you need him to be. He just wants to make you happy.

Let's hear what Jeff has to say:

I live in constant fear of being criticized for not being good enough. The truth is that I feel very average. There isn't anything wrong with me. I'm a good guy. I do well in school. I'm decent at sports. I'm good in the looks department. But I've always felt like I need to be special—to stand out from the crowd. So at a young age I started telling people what I thought they wanted to hear. It seemed to work. People liked me and wanted to be around me because I made them feel good. Now I don't even know who I am, because I've been lying for so long to make other people happy and prevent them from noticing that I'm nothing special.

Jeff is so busy pleasing the people around him so that they are too distracted to notice that he is as average as he feels. Over time, his habitual behaviors have caused him to lose sight of himself. And he doesn't have any authentic connections because he doesn't let anyone see him for who he really is. Do you find yourself trying to please others so that they will like you or not criticize you? Has the focus on making others happy led to losing your connection with who you are and what you care about?

Penina

Penina knew from a young age that in order to make her parents happy she needed to do well in school. Nothing less than straight As was acceptable. In fact, they made it clear that a B was shameful. She attended the primary school that both of her highly accomplished parents attended. And despite the fact that she was unable to do "A" work on her own, she was accepted into a very academically competitive high school. In high school, Penina felt stressed out nearly all of the time. The work was difficult, and she tried her hardest to get the perfect grades her parents wanted. So when she didn't, she felt unsuccessful and ashamed. Penina was also afraid that her friends would think the only reason she was there was because her parents had used their influence.

Let's hear what Penina has to say:

My parents are really smart and accomplished. I'm sure that I'm a disappointment to them. The highly academic school I attend is out of my league. I really struggle. Every day. With my peers and friends I act as if everything is great. But I lie about my grades because I don't want anyone to know that I'm a "B" student among all of the "A" students. At this school, it's not enough to be above average; you must be excellent. My parents pay for a private tutor to work with me every day after school. I lie to my friends about what I'm doing when I'm at home with my tutor so that they won't think I'm stupid.

Penina is trying to please her parents and fit in academically with her peers. This makes her feel like she needs to hide the parts of herself that would reveal that she doesn't have the same academic achievements as her parents and her classmates. This leaves her feeling inadequate and unworthy. Are you in an environment that forces you to compare yourself to others?

Can you identify with the struggles that Kamele, Gaia, Layla, Jeff, and Penina shared? Whether it's messages that you've received from a parent, peers, friends, or siblings or from the bigger message that is communicated—it's clear that you must be better than everyone else in order to succeed. It's a competitive world. The pressure can feel relentless: how do you compare to the other people you are competing against? The struggle starts with comparisons to others, and before long you feel that you are lacking, inadequate, flawed, unworthy, and so on. So many of the negative beliefs we have about ourselves can be linked to comparisons to others. It can be a big distraction from our own strengths and interests, and what we value. And as you may be starting to see, it makes us feel worse about ourselves. When we don't feel good about ourselves, it impacts all areas of our lives.

During this time in your life, friendships become increasingly important. But if you feel like you aren't good enough, it is difficult to do the things that are central to making and keeping friends—reaching out to others, sharing yourself authentically, and asserting your needs and expectations. If you believe that you are flawed, unworthy, lacking, or unlovable, you probably expect rejection, and this can make you miserable and vulnerable to abuse. You may believe that the people you care about will leave you or reject you if you don't behave in a certain way. Or you might fear that you will be criticized and made to feel worse about yourself if you don't put the needs of others before your own. Your beliefs about yourself might be holding you back in areas like academics and extracurricular activities (such as music, art, sports) because you believe that there's no point in challenging yourself because you are doomed to fail. Now we want you to bring some awareness to the parts of yourself that you tend to hide from others.

Try This! In the stories about Kamele, Gaia, Layla, Jeff, and Penina, they explained a part of themselves that they feel they need to hide for fear that they will be found lacking, unworthy, unlovable, or defective. In your journal, write your story about the part or parts of yourself that you hide.

How does it feel to bring awareness to the part(s) of yourself that you fear will be exposed? It's likely that you feel anxious just seeing it written out. Write about this in your journal, too.

✳ **kelly** ✳ Growing up, I remember people always referring to me as someone who's energetic, talkative, and sociable. It's true, I do love to have fun, be loud, tell stories, and so on. At the risk of sounding like I'm building myself up too much, I was often the "life of the party" as a younger kid. I love this part of myself, but it wasn't until I got older that I realized that this isn't all of who I am. Sometimes I'm energetic, talkative, and sociable, but other times I prefer to take a step back and be quieter, listen, and let other people take the reins. It wasn't until recently that I allowed myself to do that. For a while, I kept up the act of being energetic and talkative all the time because that's what I thought people liked about me. If I'm not this loud, chatty person, would my friends still want me around? I was afraid that if I was a little more shy or reserved, then I would no longer be interesting. Ultimately, I was able to bring awareness to my behavior because it was exhausting and it didn't feel authentic to me. Now, because I don't have to worry about putting on a façade, I feel like I'm a more natural and well-rounded person.

Putting It All Together

In this chapter, we've brought awareness to your beliefs about yourself and how they're formed. Our negative beliefs and distorted thoughts don't make us feel good about ourselves. In fact, they can make us pretty miserable at times or in specific situations. You probably feel worse around certain people or in specific settings, and you likely have behaviors that you feel help you cope with the increasingly uncomfortable feelings. In the next chapter, we are going to explore the people and situations that make you feel worse about yourself, so that you can start to take steps on the path that will lead you to self-acceptance and even appreciation for who you are—just as you are.

Why Do I
the Things Tha

We all know when we feel bad—we have negative thoughts, painful emotions, and uncomfortable bodily sensations. We will do almost anything to get rid of this painful experience. When you were even younger you likely tried out some behaviors to eliminate the discomfort. Maybe some were behaviors that you observed when watching your mom or dad deal with their bad feelings—for example, your mom got quiet, your dad yelled, or a sibling isolated himself or herself. Over time you likely developed your go-to behavioral reaction, and it became more automatic the more you used it. These automatic behaviors start to become so deeply entrenched that they are often outside of our awareness. Every time you're back in the same situation, with the same person or same group of people, you get triggered, and the same sequence of pain repeats: you are overwhelmed with negative thoughts, emotions, and bodily sensations. And again you react in the same or a similar way to alleviate your pain, or at least some of it.

hat these behavioral reactions usually make us
etter in the short term. Unfortunately, it's not a long-
olution, and it usually creates more problems in relation-
ips and other areas of your life. So how do you get relief from
the pain associated with particular situations, settings, people,
and events that trigger your feelings of defectiveness, unworthiness, inadequacy, and imperfection?

In this chapter, we are going to connect your feelings of
unworthiness, inadequacy, and defectiveness to the automatic
coping behaviors that you access in response to a triggering
event to make yourself feel better. It's necessary to identify
the patterns created by your beliefs and the associated behaviors in order to make the changes that will ultimately result in
your feeling better about yourself. Currently, it's likely that the
automatic behaviors connected to your beliefs are getting you
further away from what you care about and how you want to
feel about yourself.

Understanding Your Mind

First, you need to become a little friendly with your mind. It's
easy to blame ourselves for our negative thoughts and distortions. The good news and bad news is that you have less control
over your mind than you might think. Our minds are nonstop
worry machines. They are constantly on the lookout for anything that might be a threat to our survival. Your mind is a

problem solver, and it never stops looking for problems. When it can't find a problem, it can always make one up. Your mind means well; it's just trying to protect you. As you understand a bit more about how your mind works, you can more easily change your unhelpful behavioral reactions to the triggering situations that make you feel even worse about yourself.

How Your Threat Response Works

When you get caught by one of the traps or triggers (which will be detailed in this chapter), you react automatically—as if your life depended on it. There's no reason to feel bad about this reaction—it's how we are wired. At the first sign of a threat we react with fight, flight, or freeze. Your reaction is a little more emotionally powerful than what adults experience because teens are primarily ruled by their amygdala (the emotional part of the brain), while the rational part of the brain (the prefrontal cortex) is still developing. However, the amygdala plays an important role: it's largely responsible for the survival of our species. Our ancestors were constantly faced with life-threatening situations. In primal times, rejection by your tribe would have likely resulted in death from starvation or being eaten by a predator. So when you react automatically, it is usually paired with strong emotions. This happens because this part of your brain didn't get the "text message" that for the most part, when our threat response gets triggered, we don't need to react as if it's a life-or-death situation.

Identifying Your Traps and Triggers

Now we are going to explore in detail the traps and triggers associated with your beliefs about yourself and others. By bringing awareness to the people and situations that trigger your negative beliefs about yourself and result in unhelpful behavior, you will be on your way to minimizing their negative power. This exploration is the first step in helping you get unstuck from the patterns of behavior that are reinforcing the negative thoughts and beliefs that you have about yourself.

In the previous chapter, you read stories that highlight the different experiences that can make someone feel less than, unworthy, inadequate, and flawed. You identified the parts of yourself that make you feel bad and/or that you want to hide from others. Now we would like you to identify the areas of your life (we'll also refer to them as domains) that are most triggering for you.

Try This!   Read through the following list of life domains and identify the ones you find particularly challenging—meaning your negative beliefs about yourself usually get triggered. Place an "X" next to these. It's likely that you find yourself getting triggered in some areas of your life more than others. It's also possible that you are currently feeling inadequate, flawed, and unworthy in all areas of your life. There are no right or wrong answers. The solution is the same whether you check one domain, a few, most, or all of the domains.

Domains

_____   Family

_____ Friends

_____ Romantic relationships

_____ School

_____ Work

_____ Community

_____ Sports or other activities

_____ Physical fitness or appearance

_____ Social media

At this time in your life it's likely that your attention is focused on a few particular areas. As we already mentioned, developmentally the teen years are a time when friendships tend to take precedence over other relationships, so you may find that you are primarily focused on the friend domain. Again, there are no right or wrong answers. We are trying to help you bring awareness to and explore the relationship between your feelings of unworthiness, defectiveness, and inadequacy and the specific related areas of your life.

How do you feel after identifying the areas that you're struggling with right now? Did you bring awareness to an area that you might have been avoiding?

Try This! Remember the exercise in Chapter 1 where you identified the hidden parts of yourself? Now take the hidden part(s) of yourself that you identified in that exercise and write them next to the domain that is relevant.

Family:

Friends:

Romantic relationships:

School:

Work:

Community:

Sports or other activities:

Physical fitness or appearance:

Social media:

How does it feel to bring more awareness to the domains that are significant to your negative beliefs about yourself? What does it feel like to link your beliefs about yourself to specific areas of your life? Are you starting to see how it's impacting your life?

Remember Penina from Chapter 1? Here's the *SparkNotes* version: She's not feeling great about herself because of how she's doing in school. Let's take a look at how Penina completed the exercise:

Family: *My parents won't love me as much if I don't get As in school*

Friends: *I won't fit in if I'm not performing at the same level as my friends do*

Romantic relationships:

School: *I'm not smart enough to be at this school*

Work:

Community:

Sports or other activities: *I wish that I could spend more time practicing ballet, but I want to get better grades, so I have to spend my free time working*

Physical fitness or appearance:

Social media:

The point of this exercise is to keep drilling down on where and how your negative beliefs about yourself get activated. The more information you have, the more effectively you'll be able to choose new behaviors that will get you to a place of self-acceptance.

Triggering People

Now we want you to think about the types of people who tend to trigger your feelings of inadequacy, defectiveness, and unworthiness. This might mean types of people you associate with criticism and rejection.

Unpredictable: This type of person is inconsistent. Some days he/she is there for you and some days he/she isn't.

Unstable: This type of person always seems to be on the move, lacking routines or commitment.

Unavailable: This type of person is never there when you need him/her. He/she doesn't respond to texts; he/she leaves you hanging.

Detached: This type of person will not connect with you.

Withholding: This type of person will deny you the emotional connection that you need.

Judgmental: This type of person will find your flaws and expose them.

Rejecting: If this type of person finds you lacking, she/he will reject you.

Critical: This type of person will criticize you, disrespect you, and make you feel less than.

Boastful and ego-driven: This type of person will compare you unfavorably to himself/herself and others.

Clearly, an individual who engages consistently in one or more of these behaviors is a toxic person who, if you are given the choice, you would choose not to be around. But sometimes these people are unavoidable. Furthermore, almost everyone on occasion engages in one or more of these behaviors.

✳ kelly ✳ I feel triggered by judgmental people.
I think it's challenging enough to make decisions for
myself, wondering if I'm doing what's best, without
someone else on my case, telling me that I'm wrong or
bad for whatever reason.

Try This! In your journal, identify the type(s) of people who tend to trigger you the most. Can you link them to specific areas that you identified in the previous exercise?

Let's look at what Penina wrote:

Types of people: *teachers and classmates;* **Domain:** *school*

Types of people: *parents;* **Domain:** *family*

Now, can you think of any fears, statements, or themes that recur for you? Write them down next to the triggering person they relate to.

Let's look at what Penina wrote:

Types of people: *teachers and classmates;* **Domain:** *school*

I fear that I'm not worthy of being at this school; that I don't belong with my higher achieving peers; and that I'll be judged as inadequate and rejected by my peers.

Types of people: *parents;* **Domain:** *family*

I fear that I will disappoint my parents by never living up to their expectations for me and because they find me lacking I won't be worthy of their love.

Okay, that was a lot! How do you feel after bringing awareness to the areas of your life where you feel the most triggered, the people who tend to trigger you, and the fears, statements, or themes related to the triggering people?

Triggering Behaviors and Experiences

Now we want you to bring awareness to behaviors and experiences you engage in that are relevant for you. The more behaviors and experiences you can bring awareness to, the more successful you will be in making the changes that will positively impact your life and feelings of self-worth.

Try This! Let's continue to explore all of the ways that your negative beliefs about yourself get reinforced and triggered. Read through each of the following statements and put a check next to the statements that apply to you. First we'll look at behaviors—that is, actions that you engage in. Then we'll look at experiences—these are about how you feel.

Behaviors

_____ You allow yourself to be devalued.

_____ You devalue yourself (often as a preemptive strike—beating others to it).

_____ You allow yourself to be verbally, emotionally, and/or physically abused.

_____ You are hypersensitive to criticism.

_____ You react strongly to any criticism by withdrawing, or by criticizing the other person.

_____ You are constantly comparing yourself to others.

_____ You are critical of people in your life.

_____ You choose critical and/or rejecting people to be your friends.

_____ You avoid dating.

_____ You avoid social situations in which you may feel inferior or fear being seen as flawed compared to others.

_____ You reach a certain point in your relationships and pull back or withdraw.

_____ You are drawn to people who keep their relationships on a superficial level.

_____ You choose to be with people who are not high achievers.

_____ You avoid people or situations where you might be judged or criticized.

_____ You don't put the appropriate effort into your schoolwork or other activities.

_____ You minimize your accomplishments and strengths and maximize your mistakes and weaknesses.

_____ You use one aspect of yourself (appearance, personality, humor) to distract others from the ways in which you feel inadequate.

_____ You get angry at yourself when something goes wrong.

_____ You get angry at your surroundings when something goes wrong (for example, the food at a restaurant, traffic, a service person).

_____ You are constantly striving to meet high standards.

_____ You have a high level of self-control.

Experiences

_____ You live with a fear and/or a sense of dread that you will be seen only for your flaws.

_____ You feel insecure or uncomfortable around people whom you view as being flawless or less flawed compared to you.

_____ You feel insecure or uncomfortable being around people whom you fear will see you for who you really are.

_____ You feel jealous of or competitive toward others.

_____ Your relationships can feel emotionally unsafe.

_____ You feel like a fraud and live with the fear that you will be exposed.

_____ You are afraid to take on a leadership position or any role that might draw attention to you.

_____ You experience anxiety when you are around others.

_____ You regularly feel that you could have done better.

_____ You have a fear of being seen as average.

_____ You fear not being seen as the best or better than most.

_____ When you fall short of your lofty goals, you feel as if you have achieved nothing.

_____ You are unable to enjoy your life because you are constantly focused on what you haven't achieved.

_____ Whatever you achieve is never enough.

_____ You feel shame when you compare yourself to others.

_____ Despite your successes, you feel empty.

_____ You feel like you will get love and attention only if you meet high standards.

_____ You live with feelings of shame.

_____ You feel that you are not worthy of the life that you have.

_____ You feel angry or hostile toward people who seem to be getting in the way of your goals or who perform at a higher level than you.

In your journal, write down each _behavior_ statement that you identified as relevant to you. Following each statement, explain how it relates to the hidden parts of yourself and how you cope with your feelings of not being good enough. Then write down each _experience_ that you identified as relevant to you.

This exercise likely made you feel a little (or even a lot) uncomfortable because it forced you to identify behaviors and experiences that aren't pleasant. We know this doesn't feel good, but it's a necessary part of the process. Bringing awareness to your behaviors and experiences is the first step toward making different choices that will increase your feelings of self-worth and get you closer to the life that you want.

Putting It All Together

When your negative beliefs about yourself get triggered in a particular area of your life—by a type of person, a situation, or an event—you become overwhelmed with negative thoughts, painful emotions, and uncomfortable sensations. All you want to do is get rid of the pain. So it makes sense that you have behaviors that you use to help you cope with the pain and eliminate it as quickly as possible. Unfortunately, those behaviors are creating more problems for you and more feelings of inadequacy, unworthiness, and defectiveness. When you try to hide parts of yourself from others, it makes sense that you need to engage in behaviors that help you in the short term but tend to complicate and make things worse in the long term—including the way you feel about yourself. We want you to understand that this is an area where you have control, and you can make changes that will help you feel better about yourself.

In the next chapter, we are going to explore your unhelpful behaviors a bit more and assist you in making the shift to the helpful behaviors that will make you feel better about yourself. Ultimately, this will minimize your negative beliefs about yourself and make you feel good—just as you are.

chapter 3

Figuring Out What Matters to You

In the previous chapter you brought awareness to your beliefs about yourself and others. Now you probably have a better understanding about the ways in which your beliefs can drive your behaviors. Most often this works against you: rather than disconfirming your negative beliefs or making you feel better about yourself, it makes you feel worse. This creates a feedback loop in which negative thoughts and emotions lead to unhelpful behavior, which leads to feeling bad about yourself, which in turn leads back to more negative thoughts and emotions—and the vicious cycle continues.

Your behavior ends up making you feel worse about yourself because it doesn't always show others who you really are. This can be surprising because you might think of yourself as being one way, yet you end up exhibiting behavior that indicates the opposite. It's challenging to break this cycle, because our behaviors become so automatic. You are no longer making a conscious choice to respond in a particular way; instead, you are reacting in an effort to eliminate your negative emotions and thoughts. This often collides with the people and things that matter to you. And it can leave you wondering, "Wow, why did I do that? That's not who I am." Unfortunately, repeated behavioral patterns or habits define who we are. Have you heard the expression "You are what you do"? It's true. People get to know us on many levels (superficial to deep) and in many ways and situations, but the primary way in which we are judged is through observable behavior. When we "act out," we are communicating some very important information about ourselves.

We will talk more about negative thoughts and distortions in Chapter 5, but we want to emphasize that the existence of negative thoughts and distortions does not make them true. However, what can make them true, or more true, is if we *act* as if they are true. So how do you change behavior that has become automatic because of the connection to the negative thoughts and emotions that surface when you get triggered? Good question! You need to disconnect your behaviors from your thoughts and emotions and connect them to the real essence of who you are, how you want to be viewed, and what you care about.

Let's look at Kat.

Kat's Story

Kat thinks of herself as being a good friend. She would describe herself as thoughtful and caring toward her friends. Sometimes she thinks of herself as the "mama bear" of her group of girlfriends—she's always the one who has a mini bottle of spot remover in her bag when someone spills on their clothes at lunch and the ibuprofen when someone has a headache. Although she has these opinions about herself, Kat also has a core belief that she's not good enough. Often, she feels like she is not as funny, pretty, or likable as her girlfriends. When this belief—the belief that she isn't good enough—gets triggered, she can take it out on her friends by lashing out at them. Ultimately, these outbursts make Kat feel even worse, like she's *really* not good enough.

Can you relate to Kat's experience? Do you find yourself behaving in ways that make you feel worse about yourself? Are your behaviors inconsistent with what you care about?

What Do You Care About?

So, what does it look like to identify what you care about? Well, rather than reacting to the parts of yourself that you don't like and are trying to hide and defend against, you are getting in touch with what is meaningful to you, your ideal self (not a perfect self), what you value, maybe even the impact that you hope to have on the world. This can be a challenging process, because our defenses can distract us and create obstacles to our values and the things that we care about. There are a few ways to go about the process of identifying your values. We provide two exercises; one may resonate with you more than the other, but try to complete both, because this will confirm and reinforce what matters to you the most. This will guide your behavioral choices as you become more aware of how you want to live your life.

Identifying Your Ideal Self

Before we dig into the exercises, let's start by identifying and defining some qualities that are widely associated with people of high character. This will help you focus on the person you want to be and how you want others to see you. This is not an exhaustive list, so feel free to add any other qualities or characteristics that resonate with you.

* Honesty—to be honest; to tell the truth; to be truthful; to be open

* Responsibility—accepting the duty to deal with something; being accountable; the ability to act independently; a moral obligation to behave correctly and accept or take the blame when you don't

* Caring—displaying concern for others; looking after those who are unable to care for themselves

* Kindness—the quality of being friendly, generous, and considerate; having a pleasant disposition and concern for others

* Courage—the ability to do something that frightens you; strength in the face of pain

* Fairness—impartial and just treatment, or behavior without favoritism or discrimination

* Gratitude—the quality of being thankful; readiness to show appreciation for and to return kindness

* Humility—having an accurate view of one's importance in the world; modesty; lack of vanity

* Loyalty—giving or showing firm and constant support or allegiance to a person

* Patience—the capacity to accept or tolerate delay, trouble, or suffering without getting angry or upset

* Open-mindedness—being receptive and nonjudgmental and curious about other people's experiences or opinions

* Trustworthiness—the ability to be relied on as honest or truthful

* Presence—the state or fact of existing, occurring, or being present in a place or thing

* Motivation—the reason or reasons one has for acting or behaving in a particular way; a desire or willingness to do something

* Enthusiasm—feelings of intense and eager enjoyment; intense interest and enjoyment in a particular activity

* Self-respect—pride and confidence in oneself; a feeling that one is behaving with honor and dignity

* kelly * The qualities that strike me most on this list are honesty, gratitude, open-mindedness, motivation, enthusiasm, and self-respect. Honesty is important in my dealings with my family and close friends. Also, it's important for me to show others that I am thankful for them. I believe it is necessary to stay open-minded when I interact with others. Motivation is an important value because I like to work hard on things that matter to me. I love to stay enthusiastic. Lastly, self-respect is important to keep up my confidence and remember that I'm worth something (not just something—a lot!).

Discovering Values, Meaning, and Characteristics

These two exercises will help you bring awareness to what matters to you and what values or characteristics you want to connect with to bring meaning and purpose to your life.

Try This!   Think of a person or people whom you respect and/or who inspire you. What qualities do they possess? In your journal, write as many details as possible. It might be someone who is still alive or it might be an historical figure.

Let's look at the response that Sidarth wrote:

I truly respect and look up to my soccer coach, Matt. My freshman year of high school, I showed up for varsity preseason to try out for the team. I had started playing soccer only a few years before, but I loved the sport and had trained a lot that summer. When Matt introduced himself to the players, he said that what he cared most about was hard work and effort. "Talent will only take you so far," he said. While I did not end up making the team my first year, Matt would watch me play on the junior varsity team and congratulate me on how hard I was working to improve. The next year, I made the varsity team and was so excited to have Matt as my coach. He is level-headed, dedicated, and helpful, and he challenges his players. He is open to our ideas, making everyone on the team feel important and like their contributions matter.

Try This!   Imagine a group of your friends or family sitting around talking about you. What would you want to hear them say about you? What qualities of yours would you want them to highlight? Write your response in your journal.

Let's look at what Sidarth wrote:

I would want my friends and family to say that I am fun to be around, that I'm nice, that I am easy to talk to, that I give good advice and care about my friends, and that I like to try new things.

Now look back at what you wrote for each of the exercises that you completed.

Try This! As you might imagine, stating a value such as kindness sounds good, but it doesn't have any power if it isn't attached to an action—it's like the difference between a passive and an active verb. You need an action to prove that it's your value.

As you read what you wrote in the previous exercise, highlight the values or characteristics that you identified. After you've identified your values, state a behavioral intention for each value.

Let's look at what Sidarth wrote:

Level-headed, dedicated, helpful, challenging, personable, likable, thoughtful, caring, curious, adventurous, and kind

If one value you identified is kindness, then you might say being nice to others is how you can put that value into action. Now think how you can put kindness into action in specific areas of your life, such as school, friends, family, romantic relationships, and work. Identify any people or situations that make it more challenging for you to be kind.

Let's look at how Sidarth handled kindness as a value. In general he found it easy to be kind, but he had a tendency to act against his value when he was with people who were mean to him or his friends. He found himself quickly falling into the trap of behaving exactly as his mean-spirited peers were behaving. And once the confrontation or interaction was over, he was left feeling worse about himself both because of how they had treated him and because he had responded by behaving just like them. Feeling bad after you behave in a particular way is often a sign that your behavior was in conflict with your values.

Turning Values into Action

Values are what you care about and how you want to be seen. Your valued intentions are what your values look like when they are put into action. Acting on your values is one of the essential components to increasing self-worth and decreasing feelings of self-loathing. It takes practice, and it's easy to get distracted or taken off course by others, particularly if they are triggering some of the negative beliefs you have about yourself. In that situation, your first and natural instinct will be to defend yourself. It will take some time and awareness to shift from your instinctive emotional reaction to a value-based response. One way to reinforce the new behavioral choice over the habitual emotional reaction is to write down your experiences.

As we said before, Sidarth always felt worse about himself when he retaliated with name-calling. When he responded instead with valued intention, he found that, although he still felt bad about the cruel things that others said about him, he didn't feel worse about himself afterward because of what he'd done in reaction to the triggering event.

Again, we want to emphasize that this is not easy. When we are flooded with negative emotions, our automatic reaction is to do something that protects us and makes us feel better in the moment. Over time, we come to understand that it makes us feel worse in the long term, and it may actually reinforce the negative beliefs that you have about yourself.

Anna's Story

Now let's look at how Anna deals with her value of open-mindedness. Anna lives in a diverse neighborhood, and this diversity is reflected in her school community. Her friends and peers at her high school come from many different backgrounds. Her school values its diversity and promotes conversations about identity. Anna loves this about her high school experience, and she really appreciates engaging in these conversations. She is committed to hearing about others' life experiences and viewpoints.

Lately, she's found it difficult to remain open-minded in conversations with people who don't share her political view. Anna feels really passionate about one of the political candidates in an upcoming election, and she finds herself shutting people down when they criticize her candidate. In a recent conversation, Anna told a classmate that he was simply wrong and she didn't want to hear anything else he had to say. It made her feel better to shut him down in the moment. However, Anna ended up feeling really disappointed in herself that she couldn't stay open to her classmate's view.

When you have the capacity to get some distance from negative situations, you can bring more of your attention to what matters to you. What do you want to do that will add meaning to your life? This will change over time as you are exposed to more people and more experiences.

* kelly * My friends and I like to joke that when you're a teenager, particularly when you're an older teen (at least from my experience), you have a mini-existential crisis every day. During a down moment, you wonder "Am I doing this right?" or even "Am I doing this all wrong?" I feel like I often question whether I'm making the right choices, whether it's about what classes I'm taking, who I'm choosing to spend time with, how I'm spending my free time, and so on. Am I making the best out of my teenage years? What does it look like to make the best out of the time I have right now? I don't have the answers, but I feel more confident in my decisions when I let myself be open to new people, opportunities, and experiences.

Some people know at a young age what they want to do and who they want to eventually be and how they want to impact the people around them. When you can identify who and what matters to you, this, along with your values, will serve as a guide to help you live your best life. It doesn't mean that you won't get distracted or behave in ways that aren't consistent with what you care about, but you will find yourself less likely to engage in the behaviors that make you feel worse about yourself.

The Voice from the Outside

Bringing awareness to what *you* care about can be a challenging task. If you are like most teens, you have many voices coming at you with suggestions, expectations, and/or demands about what you should be doing with your life, what you need to accomplish, and how you should—or whether or not you do—measure up to your peers. This can come from parents, educators, coaches, peers, and popular culture. All of this noise can get in the way of figuring out what you truly want to do, what matters to you.

Let's hear some stories from teens about how they lowered the volume of the voices from others and got in touch with what they care about or what they want.

Bria: Parental Pressure

Bria was raised to believe that appearances mattered more than anything. Early on she understood that her father valued a good education for her, but as she got older it became obvious to her that he valued name recognition even more. The name of the school and the prestige associated with it mattered more to him than what she was learning and whether she was happy. She was compliant with his expectations for her. When she overheard him describe her, it was never about *her*; rather, it was about the schools she went to—"Bria attended Brearley, Lawrenceville, and Columbia." For him this meant that she was better than most, and because he felt that reflected on him as her father, that made him better than most, too. But something was missing for Bria. She was anxious and depressed, yet she didn't feel like she could express those challenges because they didn't fit with the image that her father needed her to project. The pressure from her father to maintain an image prevented her from developing deep relationships, because she feared showing parts of herself that weren't perfect. Toward the end of her freshman year at Columbia, she dropped out of school.

Bria didn't have an opportunity to explore and bring awareness to her values. She was too busy trying to please her father, until she couldn't do it anymore. When you are focused on pleasing others by being what they want you to be, you can lose sight of what you want. Are you distracted by the goals or expectations that your parents or others have for you?

Jackson: Peer Pressure

Jackson attended an athletics-centered high school. Jackson is a talented swimmer; he was voted to serve as one of the team's captains his sophomore year. Most of his teammates planned to swim in college, and his other friends were also going through college recruitment for the different sports they play. Even though Jackson loved to swim and was proud of how well he had done at meets in high school, he was not interested in continuing to compete at a higher level. Jackson wasn't sure what he was looking for in a college, and he wanted to have the chance to take his time to figure out what would be the best fit for him without factoring in athletics. His teammates, friends, and even his coaches told him he would be making a mistake if he didn't continue with swimming. His teammates told him he would be missing out on a once-in-a-lifetime opportunity. Jackson's coach told him that he could probably secure a partial or even full scholarship to a great college as a varsity athlete. This made Jackson wonder if he was being selfish or foolish by not pursuing an athletic scholarship. He could avoid his parents' having to put a lot of money toward his tuition, and he also could avoid taking out loans.

But Jackson just did not want to pursue a college career in swimming. He was interested in exploring other interests and groups in college and he knew he wouldn't have the time if he was on the swim team in college. Swimming was a passion of his, but he wanted to move on from it being the most important thing in his life. He considered everyone's advice, but it didn't change how he felt about his situation, and, ultimately, he recognized that it was his choice and no one else's.

Try This! Are you often distracted by the influence and expectations of others?

Write in your journal about the people who you feel try to influence your choices about your life. Who or what is a potential distraction from your values and what you care about? When you identify the people or things that are distracting you from your values, it becomes easier to recognize them in the moment and shift your attention away from the distractions and choose the value-driven action.

* kelly * A lot of people in my life try to give me advice about what I should be doing in my life. I tend to listen to the opinions of my family and my close friends about choices I'm making. They care about me, so I know their advice is coming from a good place. Also, their advice comes from an informed place—they know what I care about. I appreciate their advice, and I try to stay open to what they think, even if I don't end up following their advice. I try not to get wrapped up in what people other than my close friends and family say. Sometimes, other peers or adults will have good advice, but they don't know me as well, so at times this advice can be distracting from my values and what I want.

The Voice from the Inside

Feeling good about yourself is, in large part, an inside job. What we mean is that you need to focus on what matters to *you* and how *you* want to be seen. The messages you receive from popular culture and social media are primarily focused on how things look on the outside. These messages are a distraction from focusing on the more important core aspects of yourself. You might find yourself caught up in looking a certain way or focused on activities that don't bring long-term satisfaction or increased feelings of self-worth. It might make you feel good in the moment, but it doesn't last. You may see something on social media that makes you feel (by comparison) good about yourself, or maybe you posted something and got a lot of "likes," so you feel good. Two hours later you might see something that makes you feel bad about yourself. It's a bit like eating candy and feeling the sugar high, but unfortunately before long you crash. And it creates a cycle of addiction—you need a fix to feel better, but ultimately you always feel worse after the short-term high. It doesn't mean that you need to eliminate all of life's temporary pleasures—the sugar highs—but it does mean that you need to put them in perspective and limit your consumption of them, especially when you know that you are more vulnerable to being triggered when exposed to them. Social media enables everyone to create a false sense of accomplishment that distracts from goals that are connected to our values. For long-term fulfillment as well as greater and more stable feelings of self-worth, we must look to things like connection to others, meaning, purpose, values, and beliefs in something outside of ourselves.

Melina's Story

Melina got into an argument with a few of her close friends at school, and she felt like they were all against her. Her friends stopped texting as much in their group chat, and she assumed that they were talking in a new one that did not include her. She decided to post a photo on Instagram of herself and other friends of hers to show that she didn't need that group of friends, that she could have fun without them. When Melina first posted it, she felt great. She got a lot of likes on the picture and imagined that her friends would see it and miss her. But then when she continued not to hear from them, she got upset that she had stooped to their level. She felt even more turned against by her friends.

✳ **kelly** ✳ Whenever I'm feeling down, I know that there are specific things I can do to make myself feel better. Almost more importantly, I know that there are specific things that I can do to make myself feel much worse. Sometimes it can be easy to fall into self-destructive behavior. When I'm feeling lonely just hanging out at home, I often scroll through Facebook and Instagram, looking at my friends' photos and statuses. At first, it can be fun to look at, but then I start to feel sadder thinking about how much more fun other people are having than I am. Because I know this about myself, I try not to go on social media if I'm feeling sad or down. Instead, I'll call one of my close friends, my parents, or my brothers—someone that I'll be excited to talk to. This way, I can have a meaningful interaction with someone I love and someone who loves me. I always end up feeling better than I would if I spent time looking through social media.

You can see how these temporary distractions can negatively impact our feelings of self-worth. If we are constantly measuring ourselves against others, we are in for a roller-coaster ride. And we may find ourselves taking a perverse delight in someone else's bad experience because it makes us feel better off—in the short term. Ultimately, we feel worse about ourselves because we aren't focusing attention and energy on the things that will make us feel better—grounding ourselves in our values.

Try This! In your journal, make a list of the activities that, over time, either tend to make you feel worse about yourself or are not effective in making you feel better when you are down. After you've completed that, make a list of activities that tend to make you feel better (for example, a phone call with a close friend or family member, volunteering, exercising). You can look at this list when you're feeling down to help guide you toward making helpful choices. The choice rooted in your values might not make you feel better immediately, but it will prevent you from feeling worse and, in the long term, it will make you feel better.

Connecting and Reconnecting to Values and Character

Focusing on your character and values—how you want to behave and how you want to be perceived and experienced by others—will increase and stabilize your feelings of self-worth. This doesn't mean that you won't experience negative thoughts or feelings at times or that you won't ever behave in ways that are inconsistent with the values or beliefs that you've identified, but you will find yourself, with practice, reconnecting and reorienting yourself to the qualities and intentions that bring meaning and substance to your life.

The values that you identified can change over time. As you have more experiences and discover more about yourself, others, and your ever-expanding world, you will make adjustments to accommodate new views and goals. Bringing frequent awareness to your values will provide you with the opportunity to reevaluate (what's working and what isn't) and reprioritize (what is more important to you now).

✳ kelly ✳ I'm at a time in my life in which I feel like I'm constantly changing. In college, I'm taking classes about topics I've never learned about or even thought about before. One semester could change my entire outlook on a particular issue or subject. When I came into college, I knew that I loved working with children. I had been a volunteer at an afterschool program for elementary school students throughout high school and spent two awesome summers as a camp counselor. I started volunteering with a few organizations at my college that worked with youth. It wasn't until I started taking classes about education and educational justice, however, that I began to think about it as a primary interest of mine. After one particularly formative class, I realized that I truly valued education and wanted to pursue a career in the field of education. Once I knew I had this strong interest, I cut back on my other extracurricular commitments and focused all of my extra time outside of class on service. Now I spend a significant number of hours per week working with students or advocating for students in my local public school district.

Putting It All Together

Identifying and living your values is essential to changing unhelpful behaviors. When you act on your values, you are behaving in ways that increase your feeling of well-being and self-worth. In contrast, when you react to negative thoughts and emotions associated with triggering events, you end up damaging relationships and feeling worse about yourself. Initially, you may feel challenged to act on your values. With practice and time you will replace your automatic unhelpful behaviors with value-driven behaviors. In the meantime, keep your list of values handy, along with your valued intentions (actions), so that you have your "cheat sheet" when you need a reminder.

chapter 4

Connect to Yourself and Others

As we discussed in the previous chapter, we often try to feel better by comparing ourselves to others or, in some instances, undermining others and their achievements. This isn't a reliable, effective, or consistent solution for increasing your self-worth and self-acceptance. Instead, extensive research shows that the consistent path to higher self-worth is to practice self-compassion. Self-compassion means treating yourself as you would treat your best friend—*even* when you screw up! The great news is that you likely already know how to engage in this way of being with someone, because you probably have plenty of experience making your friends and/or loved ones feel better when they have experienced disappointment or they are critical of themselves. But, sadly, most of us don't have much experience doing this for ourselves.

Self-Compassion versus Your Inner Critic

Self-compassion might be challenging to put into practice. You've already spent time hiding parts of yourself that you don't like or feel too ashamed to let others see. And if you're like most people, you find it's easier to relate to your inner critic than to a kind voice that's attempting to make you feel better about yourself and your struggle. Think of your inner critic as the representative for your stress and anxiety. In contrast, self-compassion represents the oxytocin and other "feel good" hormones that get released when we are cared for. Self-compassion will make you feel better about yourself when you make mistakes. Your inner critic will make you feel worse.

Dealing with Your Inner Critic

It's likely that you, like everyone, has a constant companion appropriately called the inner critic. Your inner critic is rarely invited but usually shows up to highlight your imperfections, missteps, and mistakes. Your inner critic is like a narrator of your negative beliefs about yourself. And she is capable of sounding like any of the people who have ever criticized you or made cruel comments about you. She tends to keep negative past experiences alive and use them to predict the outcome of present and future experiences.

Try This! Write down the negative statements that come to mind when you get triggered by a person or people, situation, or event. You might want to refer to the triggering types of people you identified in Chapter 2. Write in your journal a description of the triggering situation along with your negative belief about yourself. Be as specific as possible.

Alicia's Story

I'm a first-generation college student. I go to a college with a strong support network for first-generation college students like me. I'm able to get advice from adults and upperclassmen who have been in my situation, and I also have a group of peers I can talk to. Sometimes, though, I still feel isolated in classroom conversations and social inter-actions. For example, recently a group of students on my dorm floor were hanging out in the common room. They were in the middle of a conversation when I walked in. All of a sudden, they stopped talking. I felt uncomfortable. I decided to ask them why they stopped their con-versation when I walked in. They told me they had been talking about the traditions at the different boarding schools they attended, and they didn't want me to feel left out, so they stopped the conversation when they saw me and planned to change to a different topic that I would be able to be a part of. I know they were trying to be thoughtful, but it made me feel bad about myself. I know I don't share their high school experience, but I can still participate in their conversation about it. It made me feel awkward about my identity and made me wonder what else they don't talk to me about.

Here's the negative statement that comes to mind for Alicia:

I feel like I'm not good enough, that other students are more cultured than I am, that other students are smarter than I am, and that I do not deserve to be here.

You have likely experienced criticism during your life—we all do. And maybe you haven't received much compassion from the people close to you. So it makes sense that you have modeled the criticism and not the compassion. You can think of criticism as the expression of a closed heart and compassion as an expression of an open heart. The shift from a closed heart to an open heart is challenging. You may have grown accustomed to protecting yourself; if so, it's natural that you automatically want to resist this process.

Having an open heart is not a constant state. Your heart will open and close depending on your experiences. When your negative beliefs aren't getting triggered it will be easier for you to practice having an open heart. You will likely not feel the need to protect yourself. You can allow yourself to be more vulnerable. Unfortunately, your negative beliefs and experiences might make you feeling like you need to be in a constant state of protecting yourself. The protective reactions might make you feel better temporarily, but they don't move you in the direction of your values. When you greet your struggles with self-compassion, you are acknowledging with kindness that you are suffering and that you are doing your best to deal with your current situation. Often our response to a triggering situation is so automatic and outside of our awareness that we don't know that we are suffering. Or you may be aware of the times that you struggle, but you greet your struggle with self-criticism.

Now let's look at how the triggering situation and subsequent negative statements can be changed by an approach rooted in self-compassion.

Developing Self-Compassion

Using the example of Alicia, we will show you how you can transform your experience and your view of it by taking a compassionate approach toward yourself while also highlighting the positive aspects that are often ignored by your inner critic.

One way to approach self-compassion is through asset-based thinking. The asset-based approach asks you to focus on your goals and the resources you have when you face a challenge or an obstacle. This doesn't mean you discount a shortcoming or negative aspect of a situation. But in order to come up with a solution and move forward, you don't focus on fixing what is broken or wrong; instead, you focus on building on the strengths that are *already* there—that exist within you. Asset-based thinkers recognize that every situation and every person has inherent value—and that includes you!

In Alicia's story, she explained that at times she feels inferior to her peers who come from higher socioeconomic backgrounds, or who have had more cultured experiences. She feels like she can't participate in certain conversations because she has different experiences than some of her peers. To be more self-compassionate, instead of thinking about what she does not have compared to her peers, Alicia would consider how her different experience could add a unique element to a conversation. When Alicia feels empowered to share her experience, she can feel like a valued member of the conversation. Further, her contributions do matter, and her peers will get to learn about her life and experiences. Alicia thinks to herself, "I have value. I am important. My experiences are interesting and matter to me. My peers are interested to hear what I have to say."

Try This!   Now that you have read our example, take your situations and statements from the previous exercise and add your self-compassionate statements. If you struggle with this process, think about what you would say to a good friend to make him see all aspects of a situation, thereby making him feel better.

Finding Connection

Often our feelings about ourselves can make us feel alone and lonely. This can lead you to hide parts of yourself, which can lead to isolation. Some of the statements we hear regularly from teens who struggle with negative beliefs about themselves are: "I feel so alone with my beliefs." "I feel like an alien." "I feel like no one else can understand how I feel—alone, separate, different, an outsider looking in." Our fear of being seen, for all that we are, can lead to more self-criticism and judgment. This separates us further from others, which leads to a distorted perception of others' experiences. When we distance ourselves from others, we can only make observations based upon superficial aspects. When you do this, it can easily lead you to the conclusion that others and their lives are more perfect than you and your life. This reinforces the impulse, need, or desire to maintain the distance or create more distance so that you aren't seen as being defective, flawed, or unworthy.

Now let's look at ways in which you can feel more connected to others.

Common Struggles

Can you remember a time when you opened up to someone or someone opened up to you about a struggle that you or they were experiencing and it brought the two of your closer? Or you felt a connection that you hadn't felt before? Write about it in your journal.

Ross's Experience

I had been dating my boyfriend, Josh, for only a few months, but we had known each other ever since middle school. In high school, we became a part of the same group of friends. Our group of friends hung out all of the time, inside and outside of school. I feel like we always had something between us, but I did not come out as gay until the beginning of my junior year. When I came out, with the love and support of my group of friends, Josh and I started hanging out more one-on-one, and soon after we decided to officially date. I was the happiest I could remember being in my life. We really cared about each other and had a lot of fun together.

After a month, I began to notice that because we were spending a lot of time together, I didn't have time to spend with other people, including my other friends and my family. I wasn't sure how to explain what I was feeling to Josh because it wasn't that I didn't love spending time together; it was just that I felt like I didn't have time for anyone else. I didn't want to talk to any of our friends about it because I thought it would put them in a weird position because they're friends with both of us. So I opened up to a girl on my debate team, Chloe, whom I'm friendly with. She's very sweet and personable, so I thought she would be happy to listen and could even be helpful. Chloe was grateful that I opened up to her and told me that she was happy that I felt I could trust her. She was very supportive and helped me come up with a way to explain my concern to Josh while still showing him that I enjoyed our time together. I left the conversation feeling confident about how to deal with my issue and feeling excited that Chloe and I had been able to connect on a deeper level.

Everyone Suffers

If you've had a similar experience, it likely involved a mix of emotions—you felt more connected to another person, but you also felt more vulnerable. You felt seen or understood, but you also felt like you shared information that could be used to hurt you, make fun of you, or expose you to others. You felt yourself and your heart open, but you had the immediate urge or impulse to close it again. You were proud of yourself for being so courageous, but also critical of yourself for being so foolish. All of these thoughts, feelings, and experiences are natural.

Sharing your experiences with others invites them to share their experiences with you. This exchange will help you understand an aspect of compassion known as common humanity. When we are suffering—experiencing negative emotions, overwhelmed by the challenges in our life—our perspective is limited because we are focused on our experience and ourselves. We are in the "I" of the storm—we can't see that everyone is suffering. All humans suffer—we are all vulnerable, mortal, and perfectly flawed. Part of embracing self-compassion is recognizing that we all suffer, we all have personal inadequacies and failings—this is part of the shared human experience. It is not just an "I" thing—it is a "we" thing. You have this in common with every person on this planet. It may look different, but the suffering is there.

First, you must bring awareness to your suffering. You might have more awareness after reading Chapters 2 and 3 and completing the exercises. However, you might be resisting bringing awareness to your suffering because you worry that it will make you feel weak. Often, people need to start with the concept of compassion before they can engage in self-compassion. With compassion you recognize the suffering in others, you wish them to be free of suffering, and you have a motivation to alleviate their suffering. When you are truly compassionate, you are vulnerable and open, and you let others see your suffering—this is how you connect to others.

As you connect to your suffering, you may experience overwhelming emotions. While this is a normal response, it will likely feel very uncomfortable and maybe intolerable. If you are having difficulty, please access your support system—a parent, a friend, a coach, a teacher, or a school counselor.

Kumail's Story

Kumail's parents put a lot of pressure on him to "keep it together" and not show his weaknesses to others. His dad told him that boys shouldn't show it when they're upset. Kumail was successful in school and had many friends, so he didn't really feel like he had many weaknesses to hide. When difficult emotions did come up, however, Kumail knew that he just needed to swallow them and put up a strong front. Eventually, he stopped acknowledging when hard feelings did come up, ignoring them altogether.

Recently, Kumail's uncle was killed in a car accident. For a long time, he hadn't let himself truly feel his emotions; when he brought awareness to what he was feeling—tremendous sadness over the loss of his family member—it was really overwhelming and painful. He wasn't sure how to handle his emotions alone.

One of his friends, Meher, noticed that he was sad and asked Kumail if everything was okay. He shared the story of his loss and talked about his emotions. She responded to Kumail with compassion—acknowledging his suffering and sharing her own experience with loss and the overwhelming emotions that can often accompany it. Kumail learned that he was not alone with his suffering. He shared his experience with another person; in turn, she shared her experience with him, thereby allowing him to see what compassion looks like. If he treated himself the way Meher treated him, then he would be practicing self-compassion.

Can you imagine treating yourself with the same warmth, understanding, and caring that you would extend to another person or they would extend to you? If so, this is a great way to access compassion and turn it toward yourself.

Dealing with What You Don't Love about Yourself

You may be feeling that you aren't going to be good at self-compassion because you can't imagine talking to yourself in a kind and loving voice. This is probably particularly true for the parts of yourself that you hide from others, the parts of yourself that you go to great lengths to avoid acknowledging because you hate them, or emotions that are difficult for you to accept. Everyone feels challenged when facing things they prefer to avoid.

That's why this exercise developed by Sharon Salzberg, in her book *Loving-Kindness: The Revolutionary Art of Happiness*, is so great. She offers an alternative meditation exercise that targets the "Difficult Aspects of Oneself." With this exercise you can create a loving-kindness meditation that is specific to you and your struggles.

Try This! In Chapter 2 you identified your beliefs, triggers, and resulting unhelpful behaviors; in Chapter 3 you identified your values and brought awareness to the distance between you and them. Review the exercises that you completed in those chapters, looking for aspects of yourself that you struggle with, and make a list. Once you have completed the list, choose four difficult aspects of yourself and write them down in a numbered list. Then create an aspirational phrase for each of them, starting with "May I ..." These phrases should connect to your struggle.

Here is an example of a loving-kindness meditation:

Difficult aspects of myself:

1. My anger

2. My fear of failure

3. My insecurity about how others view me

4. My critical self

Aspirational phrases for each difficult aspect of myself:

1. May I live with loving-kindness.

2. May I be free from fear.

3. May I celebrate my positive traits.

4. May I forgive more and maintain positivity.

Practice your loving-kindness meditation at least once a day, and pick a time of day that works best for you. You might prefer the morning, to set the tone for your day, or at night before you go to sleep, to end your day on a pleasant note.

Sharing Parts of Yourself

In our book *Communication Skills for Teens,* we discussed the process of letting others get to know you as well as the reward of self-disclosure. We know, and research backs us up, that the more we can connect to others, the better we feel about ourselves. Of course, it's important to choose the right people to share information about yourself with. Often, you don't know instantly who those people are, so we advise taking a step-wise approach to self-disclosure. Here are the eight steps to opening yourself to others.

1. *Preferences and interests.* These are things you like or dislike—for example, you hate a specific class, like trigonometry, and you love your favorite music group. This can extend to styles, places, activities, celebrities, and subjects for conversation. Even— at a more risky and brave level—things you like more or less about yourself. Sharing your tastes and

preferences can often create an instant feeling of closeness, and usually it encourages other people to share their preferences and interests with you.

2. *Information.* This is basic stuff, like which classes you take, whether you play an instrument or a sport, what you do on the weekends, what bus you take to go home, maybe the neighborhood where you live. This kind of sharing is also pretty low risk—it doesn't usually give people much of a basis to judge you, but it does give them the feeling that they're getting to know you.

3. *Your history.* At the low-risk end, this would include funny or interesting stories from your past, things that happened to you that could keep a conversation going or just be fun to share. At a deeper level, you might let others in on hard or painful things in your life—perhaps challenges or crises you had to face. While sharing struggles feels more dangerous, it's a really good way to build trust. We tend to feel safer with and closer to people who share some of the not-so-great things they've gone through.

4. *Opinions.* How you think about and evaluate things is important. Some of your opinions come from a pretty deep place within you, and they reflect how you truly see the world. Close, trusting relationships

are partly built on knowing how each of you sees things. Imagine trying to connect to someone who says nothing about what she thinks or believes. That could be uncomfortable because you'd have no clue where she's coming from. Also, it may prevent you from creating a truly meaningful connection with that person. Being willing to share some of your opinions—even on lightweight subjects—makes relationships feel safer and deeper.

5. *Values.* In the same neighborhood as opinions, but more personal and important, are your values. This is what you really care about—how you want to live your life. Values could include how you want to act and be with people you care about, what you want to do with your life, and things you feel really committed to. Values might also involve what you want for the world and what you think people should do for others. Because values often feel so important, they won't be the lead topic with a new friend. But sharing some of your values may be a big step in developing a closer relationship.

* kelly * Whenever I start in a new environment, whether it's a new job or a new school, one of my main priorities is to find people I enjoy hanging out with.

Sometimes, these people won't be lifelong friends. For example, I started a new job last year and got along really well with a few of my coworkers who were close to my age. I had a lot of fun joking around with them and hanging out both at work and in our free time. Once we started hanging out more outside of work, I started to realize that our values didn't really match up. They were really motivated to go out and party. I had fun going out with them, but I started to notice it seemed to be all they cared about. I like doing a variety of activities with my friends, not just going out. It didn't mean that we couldn't hang out anymore, but I realized the limitations of our relationship.

6. *What you want.* There are things you wanted in the past, and there are things you want for your future. It might be something simple that you wanted when you were younger—like a Lego kit for your seventh birthday. Others might be a deep yearning—like to spend more time with your brother after he moved out of your family's house. Future desires might have to do with a career, or even just the hope you don't have to take French again next year. Sharing *some* of the things you want adds depth to a relationship— and may encourage reciprocal sharing from friends. A real payoff—when friends share their desires—is that *you* feel let in. *You* feel a deeper connection.

7. *Feelings from the past.* These are the fabric of your life—moments of hope, sadness, fear, love, or anger, or even past feelings that you've had about yourself. The *good* feelings are less risky, and it usually feels safer to start there. But sharing vulnerable or painful feelings can feel like a relief—someone finally knows and understands what you went through. For these darker emotions, it is better to start with a brief mention. See if there's interest and a willingness to listen. After testing the water, you may choose to go deeper.

8. *Here-and-now experience.* This is what you feel or want *right now.* At the lower end of risk are feelings or needs relating to someone not present (not the person you're talking to). Perhaps the most difficult things to share are your feelings or needs regarding the person in front of you. This is scary; it can risk rejection. But it can change a relationship in amazing ways when your feelings and needs are finally in the open. "This has been fun, I'd like to spend more time hanging out" can trigger some painful back-pedaling if the relationship isn't going anywhere. But it could result in a closer, deeper connection if your friend wants it, too. Sharing positive feelings is challenging enough, but negative here-and-now emotions are probably the most difficult thing to

talk about. If you don't, however, and the feelings persist, they can create a silent rift that a friendship may never recover from.

＊ **kelly** ＊ Sometimes, it's easy to feel like I'm not as smart or as hardworking as other people who go to my school. Everyone takes their work very seriously, and at times it seems like everyone is busier than I am and accomplishing way more things than I do. When I keep these negative feelings to myself, they can start to really hurt me and make me feel bad. I made a new friend recently who is really thoughtful and positive. Even though we hadn't known each other for very long, I decided to talk to her about how I was feeling "less than." I told her that it was making me feel down and less motivated to do my work. I knew it was risky to express these thoughts to her—would she judge me? Would she agree that I am inferior to other people? Ultimately, this wasn't the case. I made the choice to discuss this with her because I know that she is a caring person. She totally proved me right—she listened thoughtfully and gave me reassurance that it's easy to feel like we are lagging behind when other people are succeeding, but that everyone faces challenges and no one has it together all of the time.

Sharing isn't easy for many of us. Maybe you come from a family where you were shamed, criticized, or ridiculed for being you. And you learned to hide yourself. If you come from a family like this, the risk of sharing can feel enormous.

There will be situations when you might find yourself sharing your vulnerabilities with someone without going through each of the steps. So don't worry if you skip some of the steps—it is a guide for the most cautious way to get to know someone. A more accelerated "getting to know you" process can happen during outdoor adventures, retreats, or other bonding events with people you don't know well.

✳ kelly ✳ I went on an overnight retreat organized by my school because a student in the grade above me told me she had a really great time and made a few new friends through it. I questioned whether it would actually be possible to make new friends in just one or two days, but I thought that I would try it out, because I heard good things, and it's always fun to meet new people. My friend, Sami, and I signed up together, but once we got there, we were split into different cabins and small discussion groups. At first this made me nervous, as I was with completely new people, and I had thought I would be able to have the comfort of knowing that Sami and I were together. One of the girls who stayed in my cabin, Francesca, ended up being in my small discussion group, so we ended up spending a lot of time together our first day there. We bonded quickly—first over our love of tea (she had never tried Sleepytime tea before, which I swear by) and then over more personal stuff as we began to talk about our families and our home lives. Everyone in our small group got close as we talked about some pretty personal subjects, like different aspects of our identities. Now when I see those people at school, I always smile and say hi to them. When I saw Sami later that night, I was so excited to introduce my new friend, Francesca, to her. We all got along well and have continued spending time together now that we're back at school.

As you navigate your teen years, you will find yourself in a variety of situations and circumstances that will provide you with an opportunity to be open and connect with others. Each connection you make will remind you that we all share the struggle that comes with being human. The more we can practice compassion toward ourselves as well as others, the more it will ease some of the suffering that is part our lives.

Putting It All Together

Self-compassion is a game-changer when it comes to increasing feelings of self-worth. Treating yourself with understanding and kindness when you are facing difficult times or following a screw-up will allow you to be more open, thereby making it easier to connect with others. When you don't practice self-compassion, you will likely feel alone, isolated, and separate from other people. When you fail (and we all do), if you greet your failure with self-compassion (i.e., "I'm like everyone else" and "This is a normal part of everyone's experience") rather than self-criticism (i.e., "I'm awful" or "I suck"), then your feelings of self-worth will remain much more stable over time because you are being kind to yourself and judging yourself positively.

chapter 5

Mindfulness and the Monkey Mind

While we want to feel good about ourselves *now*, in our minds, we tend to be everywhere but in the *now*. We are more often ruminating about the past or predicting and worrying about the future. A regular mindfulness practice will create a habit of attention. It will change your relationship with your mind, your thoughts, and yourself. Why is this important to you? When your negative beliefs get triggered, you are instantly transported back in time. This means your perceptions become limited by your past experience. Your ability to judge the current situation is altered; your reaction is automatic, and it usually happens before you even have a chance to think about it. You are no longer judging the current situation—your mind is using old information from the past to reach a conclusion, and your view of the present is distorted.

This chapter will explain the important role of mindfulness as a part of self-acceptance. Mindfulness can help prevent reactions to past experiences by staying with the current experience when your negative beliefs about yourself get triggered. Our thoughts can be a powerful distraction from our present experience. Mindfulness can help you create a new relationship with your thoughts and help keep you present with your experiences.

Mindfulness and Thought Patterns

Can you imagine allowing the current information to enter your mind, observe what's happening with acceptance rather than fear, and respond with a valued intention rather than the automatic reinforcing behavior that's linked to your negative beliefs? This is the difference between our usual way of doing things and a mindfulness approach.

It's likely you've heard about mindfulness, or maybe you've experienced the practice in a school or recreational setting. It's proven as an effective approach to combat a variety of conditions, including anxiety, depression, eating disorders, PTSD, and more. The research is abundant supporting the use of mindfulness and meditation practices to increase health and well-being. However, many find it challenging—it's not unusual to hear "I'm not good at it," "It's not for me," "I can't stop thinking about stuff," and so on. If you can identify with any of these statements, you are not alone. These are real and valid experiences. We are all challenged by the concept of being in the moment and truly experiencing what is happening right now.

* kelly * Last semester, one of my professors paired up with the university's counseling services department to incorporate well-being and reflection into the course. One day, one of the school psychologists came into class to speak with us about well-being in college. He began the session by asking us to identify sources of stress in our lives, and then we listed strategies we use to manage the stress and care for ourselves. Next, he introduced mindfulness and meditation as a way to care for ourselves and prioritize our well-being. The psychologist explained that mindfulness is paying attention in a particular, purposeful way. Meditation is one way that we can improve mindfulness—it's a way that we can change our relationship with our thoughts. Then, it was our turn to try to meditate for one minute as we sat at our desks. To be honest, it felt a little awkward and unnatural to meditate in a class setting. Still, I tried my best to bring awareness to the present during that minute, and I felt like it was something I would be willing to try again.

Before we go any further, let's explain mindfulness. Simply put, it's bringing awareness to the present moment while acknowledging and accepting your thoughts, emotions, and bodily sensations *without* judgment. That might sound easy (or not), but we are often not present in the moment. Have you ever been in a classroom or other group setting or situation where the teacher, coach, or leader is calling names to see who is present? Your name is called, you respond "Here," but you're actually only physically there—your mind is generating thoughts about what you want to eat for lunch, a movie that's opening this weekend, or what you're going to get your best friend for her birthday. Your mind is a nonstop thought machine that you can never turn off.

Understanding how you relate to your mind and the thoughts it generates is helpful to adopting a mindfulness practice. Typically, the majority of thoughts are ruminations about the past or worries about the future. Maybe you don't believe this to be true for you. One of our favorite exercises to test the truth of this statement is the three bowls exercise (by Randy J. Paterson, PhD, in his book *How to Be Miserable*).

Try This!

1. Place three bowls in front of you in a row.

2. Use 3x5 cards or small pieces of paper to write down each thought as it comes into your mind. Use the bowl on your right for thoughts about the future. Use the bowl on your left for thoughts about the past. And use the bowl in the center for thoughts about the present.

Spend at least fifteen minutes on this exercise. As your mind generates a thought, write it down and place it in the appropriate bowl. Continue to do this for each thought. After fifteen minutes you can stop. Now look at the bowls. If you're like most of us, the bowl in the center has the fewest

3x5 cards or pieces of paper. Don't judge yourself. It's expected. This is the natural tendency of the mind. That's why mindfulness can be or is so challenging.

✱ kelly ✱ This exercise was particularly challenging for me. The bowl in the center had very few cards. The majority of the cards were in the "future" bowl. Right now, I'm focusing a lot on what career path I might want to pursue after college, and how I can successfully prepare myself to get a job. So it makes sense that my thoughts are more future-focused at the moment. What I took away from this exercise is that I'd like to channel this energy into the present. I recognize that it is important to think about my future and what I want from it—one way that I can achieve my goals is to think about what I can do in the present to work toward what I want. What can I focus on right now that will serve me in the future? One idea: I'll focus on my schoolwork and seek out opportunities to explore my academic interests in new ways.

Try This! Now we want you to take your thoughts from the bowl on the left—your thoughts about the past—and link each of those thoughts to one of your beliefs about yourself that you identified in Chapter 1. Pick one or two of the beliefs that are most relevant for you.

Let's take a look at what Harry wrote:

Thoughts about the past:

1. *I spent so much time thinking about what other people in my life wanted instead of what I wanted.*

2. *I should have gotten much better grades in high school.*

3. *I wish I had spent more time with my grandparents before they passed away.*

Beliefs about myself:

1. *Other people's needs are more important than mine.*

2. *I'm not good enough.*

3. *I'm not a good person.*

Next, complete the same exercise with the thoughts from the bowl on the right.

This is what Harry wrote:

Thoughts about the future:

1. *I don't know if I will ever find a career that I am interested in.*

2. *I don't know if I will ever fall in love.*

3. *I am worried that I won't meet my parents' expectations for me.*

Beliefs about myself:

1. *I'm a failure.*

2. *I'm not lovable.*

3. *I'm not good enough.*

Are you beginning to see how your thoughts about your past (usually in the form of ruminations or regrets) and your thoughts about the future (usually in the form of worries and fear) reinforce your negative beliefs about yourself? The less we are present in the moment, the more time we spend in the feedback loop that reinforces our negative beliefs about ourselves. Every time we bring ourselves back to the moment, we break that cycle.

You might be wondering if there is something that you can do about your thoughts. If only you could stop your mind from generating so many unhelpful thoughts! Unfortunately, you can't control your mind, but the good news is that you can change your relationship with your mind. That is the transformative power of mindfulness.

What does this mean? As a thought enters your mind, you observe it in a curious, nonjudgmental way. You don't attach to it or take it as the truth. You identify it for what it is, and you let it go. If you hang on to it, you are getting dragged back to the past or pulled into the future; you are not in the present. Living in the past or the future creates unnecessary stress and emotional pain and prevents you from bringing awareness to what is happening in the moment.

Let's look at the way in which your relationship to your thoughts has negatively impacted you.

Try This!   How have your thoughts defined you? How have they influenced who you think you are? How have they guided your actions and behaviors? Think about at least one specific example and write about it in your journal.

How do you feel after completing this exercise? Are you able to see how attaching to your thoughts can reinforce your negative beliefs about yourself? Can you recognize the power that you give your thoughts by treating them as facts and using them to reinforce your negative beliefs and influence your behaviors?

✳ kelly ✳ I love to exercise—it makes me feel good and is often a good distraction from school- or friend-related stress. I've always been intimidated by running, though. I have this belief that I am not good enough to run because it's not my regular workout activity. I think about my mom—she runs every single day. I then compare myself to her and believe that I can't run because I don't do it every day like she does. This belief prevents me from doing something I might enjoy because of my thoughts about my mom's running ability and my running ability. In making this comparison, I'm not giving myself enough credit. The truth is that I likely am capable of running regularly. (Still haven't started, though—check back with me on that one.)

Mindfulness helps us let go and stop attaching. When you recognize the impermanence of your thoughts, emotions, and sensations, it can be very powerful. It almost seems too simple. But when we feel stuck, as you probably do right now, everything seems permanent—the thoughts "I'm flawed" or "I'm unworthy," the feeling of loneliness, and the ache in the pit of your stomach. But the reality is that every thought, every emotion, and every sensation has passed with time. They have come and they have gone.

By attaching to our negative beliefs and the resulting thoughts, we come to believe that they define who we are at our core. In turn, our inner self is expressed through our outer self. That is how our negative beliefs get reinforced and continue to cause us additional pain. So we need to develop a different relationship with our mind. You know that your mind is part of you, but it's not all of you. The thoughts that are produced by your mind are based on your experiences. And they are largely out of your control, although you might be feeling like they control you. With mindfulness, you don't attach to your thoughts. Instead, you create distance from your thoughts; you become an observer of your mind. Your mind is doing what it was designed and evolved to do—it is trying to protect you by judging situations and predicting danger based on past experiences. But our minds aren't perfect; they tend to be overly cautious, and that can get us into trouble, especially if we are faced with a situation or person that triggers a negative belief.

Are you convinced now that it would help you to adopt a practice that will allow you to change your relationship with your mind? Can you see the connection between your relationship with your mind and the degree of suffering you experience?

Your negative beliefs can distort your perception of reality. By staying in the moment, you are better able to see things as they really are in … this … moment. No fortune-telling, no alarmist prediction, no fears of catastrophes.

When you can create distance between yourself and your thoughts, you can connect more deeply with what and who is in your *now*. When your negative beliefs get triggered, you experience thoughts that are related to your fears. There are probably some that you've had so often you have them memorized. Other thoughts might be new to you, but they are likely familiar, in that they come from a need to be safe and protected.

Now we'll look at the thought patterns that can drive your unhelpful behavior, thereby reinforcing your negative beliefs.

Try This! In Chapter 2 you identified situations, domains, and types of people who trigger your negative beliefs about yourself. When you get triggered, it's likely that each time you have the same or similar thoughts. Now you're going to bring them to awareness so that you can create distance between yourself and these thought patterns. Start by listing typical situations or experiences that trigger your negative beliefs and the recurring thoughts associated with them.

When you are finished, read back through your list and look for patterns. Did you find any?

Can you see how identifying with your thoughts in specific triggering situations and/or experiences is creating additional suffering?

Your thoughts are thoughts. Your thoughts are not you. But we often get lost in our thoughts, especially when they are related to our negative beliefs. It's easy to see how they become so powerful and such a dominating presence that we treat our thoughts as factual evaluations of who we are.

Jordan's Thought Patterns

Let's look at what Jordan wrote for her thought patterns when she is triggered in her romantic relationship domain:

* *He's going to see someone he thinks is better than me.*

* *He's going to meet someone better than me.*

* *He doesn't really like me.*

* *He thinks I am annoying and not fun to be around.*

* *I am flawed, and he thinks no other girls would act the way I do.*

* *I am not good enough for him.*

* *I am not worthy of, or can't sustain, a long-term relationship; the real me will come out.*

* *If he sees someone he thinks is prettier than I am, I will disappear or mean less to him.*

* *He doesn't really want to hang out with me but feels like he has to.*

As you read Jordan's negative thought patterns, can you imagine how they might drive her to act as if they were true? Let's look at Jordan's triggering event and her reaction.

Triggering event: *Ethan didn't immediately respond to my text.*

Thoughts: *I'm not good enough. He doesn't really like me. He doesn't want to hang out with me. He's probably with a girl who is better than me.*

Behavioral reaction: *I sent a bunch of text messages accusing him of being with someone else and not liking me as much and I canceled plans that we had for the upcoming weekend.*

Here's what Jordan wrote about what really happened with Ethan:

The reality was that Ethan had left his phone in his mom's car and she was at a business dinner, so he couldn't reach her. When Ethan finally got his phone and read my text messages he was shocked and hurt. We had just started dating and he liked me, but after my awful texts he said he couldn't be with someone who would say such mean things to him. So, he broke it off with me. Now, I feel even worse about myself, and it makes my negative thoughts feel more true.

It's easy to see how attaching to these negative thoughts could result in a behavioral reaction that would be unhelpful and would likely reinforce Jordan's negative beliefs about herself.

Now bring awareness to what this would look like for you.

Try This! Take the information from the preceding exercise and add your behavioral reaction. In other words, how would you react if you were in your triggering situation and you were getting caught up in your associated thought patterns? Can you see how viewing your thoughts as facts influences your behavior and creates more problems or makes you feel worse about yourself?

How does it feel to bring awareness to the connection between thoughts and behaviors?

It's likely that the triggering situation, the associated thoughts, and the behavioral reaction all happen so quickly, so automatically, that you have limited awareness about what is happening in the moment. The goal is to switch from autopilot to mindfulness.

When you can bring attention to your present experience without attaching to your thoughts you will increase your ability to make a behavioral choice that is consistent with your values. It is helpful, when switching from automatic behaviors to value-driven behaviors, to identify what the value-driven behavior would be for a triggering situation (we will dig deeper into this in Chapter 7). These helpful behaviors will replace your current unhelpful behaviors. As a result, your feelings of self-worth will increase.

The Autopilot Switch

You may already recognize that the autopilot switch gets turned on when you are engaging in a familiar or routine task or activity—riding the bus to school, making your bed, brushing your teeth, and so on. You've engaged in the activity so many times that you don't bring as much awareness to it as you did when you were doing it for the first time. Can you identify some activities that you tend to do without really thinking about it?

✳ kelly ✳ When I started driving, I paid such close attention to every decision I made. I would get in the car, check that everything in the car was set correctly, and focus intently on the task of driving as I traveled to my destination. If I had to turn left in two blocks, I would begin observing my surroundings, using my mirrors and looking out my window, turn my signal on at the appropriate time, and carefully turn onto the street. I didn't think about other things, like what might happen when I got to school or got home. I completely dedicated my mind to the task at hand.

A few years after I got my license, I was no longer so intentional about my driving. I've driven to my best friend Joanna's house at least fifty times, so I am super familiar with the route—I think I even know the timing of the stoplights. Recently, when I parked outside her house and turned my car off, I realized that I hadn't really thought about what I was doing the whole time. I took for granted that I knew the directions so well that I didn't even focus on driving. I couldn't even remember what I had thought about instead. It made me feel nervous—what if something unusual had happened? I was thankful, of course, that I had gotten there safely. But I resolved that when I drove home, I would focus on the road.

Now, can you think about a recent experience in which you had to really focus in order to complete the task or participate in the activity? This could have been learning a new game or sport or spending time with someone new or visiting a place you've never been to before. These more novel or new experiences require you to focus more of your energy in the moment. Your memories of the experience might be more powerful. You might feel more engaged.

✳ kelly ✳ Recently, my good friend Erin introduced me to a friend of hers I had heard about but hadn't met before. It's so easy for me to get into routines in which I spend time with the same people (whom I love—don't get me wrong!) and not put myself out there. So I was excited to meet someone new and open myself up to the opportunity of having a new friend. When I met up with the girl to grab lunch, I realized that I couldn't default to the way that I act in an everyday hangout with a close friend. This was someone who hadn't met me before, and I needed to make an effort to engage with her. I brought all my focus to that interaction. I didn't think about my phone that was buzzing, or my upcoming Spanish exam. I had fun spending time with someone without thinking about other things. It felt really good!

Mindfulness Practices

Practicing mindfulness will train you to let your thoughts go. Whether the thought brings a smile or a frown to your face, you just let it go—you don't attach to it. You might be wondering why you can't attach to a thought that makes you feel good. While it sounds like a pleasant experience, the problem is that we will just as easily attach to a thought that makes us feel bad, especially when one of your negative beliefs has been triggered. So we practice not attaching to any thought.

Now we want to introduce you to some mindfulness exercises that will help train you to bring your awareness to the present moment. Remember, this is not easy, and it takes practice, so don't judge yourself if it takes you more time than you thought it would.

Try This! This exercise is a step toward observing your current situation for what it is, without your negative beliefs distorting it. This will allow you to give your thoughts and feelings their moment and see them for what they are—temporary experiences that don't require a behavioral reaction. Read the exercise first to become familiar with it, and then give it a try. (You can also find a recording of this exercise at www.kellyskeen.com.)

> *Close your eyes and take a deep breath ... and notice the experience of breathing. Observe, perhaps, the feeling of coolness as the breath passes the back of your nose or down the back of your throat ... And notice the sensation of your ribs expanding, the air entering your lungs ... And be aware of your diaphragm stretching with the breath, and of the feeling of release as you exhale. Just keep watching your breath, letting your attention move along the path of flowing air ... in and out ... in and out. As you breathe, you will notice other experiences. You may be aware of thoughts; when a thought comes up, just say to yourself, "Thought." Just label it for what it is: thought. And if you're aware of a sensation, whatever it is, just say to yourself, "Sensation." Just label it for what it is: sensation. And if you notice an emotion, just say to yourself, "Emotion." Just label it for what it is: emotion. Try not to hold on to any experience. Just label it and let it go. And wait for the next experience. You are just watching your mind and body, labeling thoughts, sensations, and emotions. If something feels painful, just note the pain and remain open to the next thing that comes up. Keep watching each experience, whatever it is, labeling it and letting it pass in order to be open for what comes next.*
>
> *Let it all happen as you watch: thoughts ... sensations ... emotions. It's all just weather, while you are the sky. Just passing weather ... to watch ... and label ... and let go.*

Meditate silently for another two minutes, and finish by opening your eyes and returning your attention to your surroundings.

We encourage you to do this mindful-focusing exercise once a day so that you become comfortable with observing your inner experience without engaging in a behavioral reaction. By being mindful and remaining aware of the flow of your current experience, you can gain the distance from your past experiences that will allow you to respond with flexibility to each situation rather than viewing each triggering event in the same way and reacting with the same unhelpful communication style and behavior. Observe your current experience and the accompanying emotional pain without judging it or trying to stop or avoid what is happening to you in the moment. With this distance, you can be curious and open about your current experience. And you will be able to see more behavioral options. You may still have the same thoughts, sensations, and emotions, but you will respond to them differently.

Bringing More Awareness to Your Present Experiences

Mindfulness activities help you stay in the moment with your sensory experience. Mindfulness—the ability to observe each moment—isn't just about watching your inner experience; it's something you can learn through everyday activities. Instead of doing them in your usual autopilot mode, you can perform these tasks with full awareness. When thoughts come up, and they will, you can note them and return your attention to your five senses.

Here are a few suggestions for mindfulness activities. Add your favorite activities to the list.

Mindful drinking and eating. We love this activity for a morning cup of coffee or tea, but you can do it any time. While you're enjoying your favorite beverage, notice the liquid in your mouth, the temperature, the smell, the taste, the feelings in your throat and stomach as the liquid goes down, the weight and temperature of the cup. Bring awareness to all aspects of your experience.

* **kelly** * I was recently told to bring more mindfulness to my meal experiences. Often, I watch TV or read the news on my phone or computer while I eat a meal, not focusing on the physical act of eating. More recently, I've been trying to only eat while I eat—I put away my phone and computer and focus on enjoying my meal. It's been helpful in that I have a set time when I'm disconnected from technology, and also I'm more aware of what and how much I'm eating.

Mindful bathing or showering. This is a great activity because your entire body is exposed to all of the sensations. Notice the temperature of the water, the sensations as the water meets your skin, the feel of the soap or bubbles against your skin, the smell of the soap, the noise of the water. Bring awareness to all aspects of your experience.

Mindful walking or running. We love this mindful activity because there is so much to bring awareness to: the pressure on your feet when they meet the pavement, the sound of your breath, the smell of the outdoors, the noises you hear as you pass people or as cars pass you, the feeling in your arms and hands as you move them. Bring awareness to all of your sensory experiences.

The goal for mindfulness activities is to stay with your sensory experience. Don't fight your thoughts when they pop up—just acknowledge them and turn your attention back to your five senses.

Doing one or more mindfulness activity each day strengthens the skill of self-observation. It will train you to notice your experience moment to moment and accept the experience for what it is without judgment. These activities do not need to take a lot of time. They are meant to be brief opportunities for you to practice being in the here and now.

Here are some other mindfulness activities: putting together jigsaw puzzles, painting by numbers, or coloring with pencils, markers, or crayons. A friend does needlepoint as her mindfulness activity, and knitting is another popular mindfulness activity. Pick something you enjoy so you will want to do it more often.

✳ kelly ✳ Over winter break, I was home and saw my mom getting really into jigsaw puzzles as a mindfulness activity. At first, I was intimidated to try it because it seemed difficult and I was unsure I'd be able to focus on it for an extended period of time without giving up. Then my best friend Joanna and I found a puzzle at her house and gave it a try. I loved it—I was able to dismiss stressful thoughts that had been weighing down on me and focus on the present activity. Plus, we felt so successful and proud of ourselves when we completed it! I even posted a picture of the finished puzzle on my Instagram.

The Role of Gratitude

When you're struggling and you feel consumed by your problems and your painful emotional experience, it's difficult to bring attention to what is good in your life. What do you appreciate? What are you grateful for? It can even sound like one of these ridiculous feel-good self-help strategies. But there's a lot of evidence to support the positive role of gratitude—even more so if you are stuck in a place where it feels as if everything is wrong.

✳ kelly ✳ Recently, at work, I was speaking with one of my coworkers whom I consider to be a friend. He seemed really upset, so much so that it was difficult to even have a casual exchange with him, so I took him aside and asked him how he was doing. It turned out that he had recently broken up with his boyfriend. When he began talking about it, I could tell that he was super overwhelmed and upset. He told me that everything was bad, that he was so unhappy, and on and on. I validated his pain, but then I asked him how his winter break was with his family. He said it was great. I asked him how his friends were. He told me it's been great to be back at school and spend time with his friends, that he missed them over the holidays. I asked him how his job search was going, and he told me that he had just accepted a job that he was very excited about. We continued to talk about all of the great things that were happening in his life, and I reminded him of all that he has to be thankful for. The next time that I felt like one aspect of my life was negatively affecting how I feel about everything, I thought about this interaction, and it reminded me that in a difficult time, I should reflect on all of the amazing things in my life!

Gratitude is a natural antidepressant. Bringing awareness to the things that we are grateful for increases production of dopamine and serotonin. It's a natural way to get some of the same effects as some prescription medications provide—without the side effects. The more you practice gratitude, the more you activate the neural circuits, and the stronger the neural pathways become. What we pay attention to begins to grow. This means fighting our natural negativity bias and shifting our attention to look for what is going right. With time, our brains get trained to look for more positive things instead of looking for problems or what's going wrong. The other benefit to practicing gratitude is that it brings more of our attention to the present moment.

Try This! Bringing attention to the moment, as well as to the positive aspects of your life and your day, produces short-term and long-term benefits by increasing your feeling of well-being.

Complete the following exercise each day. Write in the style that is comfortable for you. Use the statements as prompts for your daily gratitude.

You may find yourself writing the same things for several days. That's good. You don't need to have different things each day. But try to bring awareness to even the small things that can make a big difference in your day. By focusing on the positive, you are turning your attention away from what tends to reinforce your negative beliefs, and toward people and events that make you feel better and improve your life.

* **kelly** * Here's what I wrote:

#1

I'm grateful for: my supportive, tight-knit family.

My role in it was: putting in the effort to strengthen my relationships with my brothers, mom, and dad.

When I think about it, I feel: content now and excited for what lies ahead for us as a family.

#2

I'm grateful for: my body—the ability to exercise, move, and sweat.

My role in it was: taking care of my body—getting sleep, eating well—so that it can do all of the amazing things it does.

When I think about it, I feel: proud of what I can accomplish.

#3

I'm grateful for: my education.

My role in it was: working hard and taking advantage of the opportunities that were provided to me.

When I think about it, I feel: lucky for everything that I have access to as a college student and educated person.

I have to say, I love gratitude exercises. On challenging days, I wake up, and I think about one thing that I am really proud of about myself, one thing I am really good at, and how that can serve me today. That helps me start my day on a positive, productive note.

We've asked you to spend some time bringing awareness to your negative beliefs, and to the behaviors that often reinforce those beliefs, so that you can better understand your obstacles in an effort to overcome them. Right about now, you might be feeling like you've drawn attention to more of the negative aspects or influences in your life, including people. So let's take some time and bring awareness to the people, past and present, who have been a positive influence in your life. It might be someone you never thanked, or someone you want to thank in more detail, or it might be someone you see every day. You do not need to send the letter. Research indicates that the process of writing the letter increases your feeling of well-being.

Try This!   Write a letter of gratitude to someone who has brought joy to your life. After you write the letter, reflect on the process and record your experience in your journal. Did writing it make you feel better?

* kelly * At the end of the school year, I felt so thankful for one friend in particular, so I decided to write her a letter to express how much I appreciate her as a person and our friendship. I could have easily sent my note as a text or a Facebook message, but I wanted to mail it—it felt extra special to send it the old-fashioned way. I took out stationery, found a nice inky pen, and wrote freely about our relationship and our great memories together. It made me feel so happy. It made me feel even more thankful for her. I was even excited to address the envelope and walk it to the mailbox. The process made me feel super in touch with my emotions and my state of being.

Putting It All Together

Mindfulness, like self-compassion, is a game changer. When you can stay in the moment with your experience, observing your thoughts, emotions, and bodily sensations without judgment, you are better able to accept your experience for what it is. This will enable you to make behavioral choices that are consistent with your values rather than engaging in automatic behavioral reactions that reinforce negative beliefs. And the practice of mindfulness will help you avoid getting stuck in thoughts of regret about the past, or in fearful, worrying thoughts about the future. Without those distractions, you can bring more awareness to what you are grateful for in your life.

In the next chapter, we are going to look more closely at our emotions, specifically, our relationship with emotions and how—if we let them—they can negatively influence behavior and reinforce negative beliefs.

chapter 6

Emotions and the "I" of the Storm

Emotions are a powerful force that fuels our thoughts and behaviors. As you were growing up, you may have received messages about emotions—which ones are acceptable and which ones aren't. We all have opinions about emotions—we often categorize them in terms of good emotions and bad emotions. Or we find some emotions more tolerable than others. Did you see the 2015 animated movie *Inside Out*? The movie does a great job of showing the importance of all of our emotions. For the purpose of simplification and time constraints, the filmmakers only picked five emotions—anger, sadness, joy, fear, and disgust. When we're talking about our negative beliefs about ourselves, we can certainly identify fear as a primary emotion. Fear that others will see our faults, fear of rejection, fear of failure, and fear of not being good enough. Our emotions guide us in our interactions with others as well as how we view current and past situations. This means that our perception is colored or distorted by the emotion that is present at the time of the viewing. And when your negative beliefs get triggered, your emotions take over and hijack your mind. This is called an amygdala hijack. The amygdala is located in the "seat" of the brain, and it's more active in teens because the prefrontal cortex is still developing. This explains why teens tend to be more emotional in this developmental stage.

Your negative beliefs about yourself and your imperfections often lead to hiding or rejecting parts of yourself that you don't want others to see or that make you feel worse about yourself. What you try to hide or reject can include your emotions. This, in part, explains why certain emotions are difficult for us to tolerate. Many times we are discouraged from expressing our full range of emotions and shamed if we do express them. Some of us have parents who aren't emotionally expressive. This often means that we never really learn how to identify, process, and express emotions in a healthy and productive way. We might even internalize the rejection of emotions as a rejection of us. Our feelings are bad, we conclude, and that makes us bad; when we hear that certain feelings don't matter, it can understandably make us feel that *we* don't matter. By rejecting some of the emotional parts of ourselves, we are often left feeling empty and ill-equipped to deal with emotional pain.

This chapter will explain the power of emotions— particularly negative emotions that result from belief-triggering events, people, and situations. A greater understanding of what is happening with your emotions in the moment and how to tolerate the discomfort will make it easier for you to behave in ways that move you closer to your values.

> ✳ **kelly** ✳ One emotion I find particularly hard to deal with is stress. When I am stressed about something in particular—about a school assignment or an exam, or about an issue with someone in my family or a friend—it's difficult for me to compartmentalize that feeling. I feel like my stress affects every other part of my life. I also feel embarrassed to admit that I'm feeling so stressed and overwhelmed when I know that my friends and peers are all dealing with their own school commitments too, and it can seem like they're managing their stress well, or at least better than I am.

It's challenging to manage the powerful emotions that are generated by negative triggering experiences. The threat response when your negative beliefs are triggered creates an intense impulse to take action to get rid of them. The anxiety you experience serves a survival function—when you are faced with a threat or dangerous situation, it will shift you into a fight, flight, or freeze mode. When your negative beliefs gets triggered, you probably experience a high level of anxiety—this, in turn, activates fear. Although you often experience anxiety and fear together, they are two distinctly different emotions. Anxiety prepares you for what might occur in the future, whereas fear is a reaction to an immediate threat or danger. The physical sensations are probably familiar to you—your heart rate increases; your feet and hands may become cold, tingly, or numb; your breathing is faster and more labored; you may feel like you can't catch your breath, like someone is sitting on your chest; your mouth may be dry; or you may feel like you are going to be sick to your stomach. You have an urge to act immediately to get rid of the threat and your uncomfortable emotions and sensations.

In some situations, and certainly historically, acting on this impulse is adaptive. You are facing a lion—it's kill or be killed. A modern example might be swerving to avoid crashing into a vehicle that's coming toward you. But the emotions we experience when our negative beliefs get triggered feel intolerable, and we feel as if we need to react quickly to eliminate the threat, because it feels life threatening, even if it's not.

The Emotional Whiteout

Bringing awareness to these intolerable emotions and understanding their function is an important step in learning how to deal with them. We need all of these emotions in order to experience life fully, so it's necessary for us to learn how to deal with them. While our emotions may make us feel bad at times, they aren't the problem. Our behavior in reaction to them is what can create problems. When negative beliefs get triggered, it creates an emotional storm that can feel overwhelming. This emotional storm often blinds you to everything else that is around you.

Imagine the whiteout that occurs during a blizzard when you can't see anything due to the wind and snow. You've probably seen images on the news of instances in which people have continued to drive despite low visibility—cars have run off the road, there are multi-car pileups. The same thing happens, figuratively, when we are blinded by our emotions.

An emotional whiteout occurs when your negative beliefs get triggered and you're flooded with emotions and associated thoughts and sensations—you become blind to your current situation. At the same time, you have an urge to react quickly, as if it's a threat that you need to eliminate. Unfortunately, you are temporarily blind to what is going on in the present. Your behavioral reaction to the overwhelming emotional experience is usually not helpful. And it usually leaves you feeling worse about yourself.

Cary's Story

Let's look at Cary's story as an example of how the mishandling of our emotions can play out.

Cary lived with one of her closest friends, Antonia, during their first year of college. Now it was their sophomore year and because they no longer lived together their relationship and the frequency of their interactions had changed. It was a real challenge for Cary to express her needs and emotions when she felt like she wasn't spending as much time with Antonia as she needed. The following is a list of her experiences following a period in which Cary felt that Antonia had been too busy to spend time with Cary.

* Upset that we had not spent time together for weeks

* Feelings of not being as connected and close anymore

* Unhappy that she made no extra effort to see me when she was busy

* Yearning for the better times between us, but not knowing how to bring them back

* Feeling of loneliness and being alone

Cary had not fully expressed any of these feeling to Antonia. Clearly, her frustration and a range of emotions were building and the experience was triggering her negative belief that she wasn't good enough. Finally, Cary and Antonia made a plan to spend quality time together—beyond just seeing each other in passing on campus. That night, they planned to go out to a movie and try a new restaurant, but Antonia had some last-minute work to do on an assignment for class. Cary experienced this as another sign that for Antonia, everything and everyone took priority over her and their friendship. Her emotional storm was building. As soon as she saw Antonia, she felt overwhelmed with emotion—the whiteout had hit! She couldn't see or hear anything that was happening in the present moment. At the time, she didn't recognize what was happening. She lashed out at Antonia. She told her how awful she was and that she didn't want to be friends anymore. She blew up their friendship within a matter of minutes. In the moment, Cary felt better that she was releasing all of the painful emotions she was experiencing. Antonia was stunned and very upset. From her perspective, she almost wondered if Cary was on drugs or some mind-altering substance, because she was not acting like the friend she knew so well. Antonia tried to reason with Cary, but it was impossible to get through to her.

The next morning, the emotional storm had passed and Cary could see clearly. Here is what she wrote:

* I feel awful (always do after an outburst).

* Regret about what I said to Antonia

* My inability to communicate appropriately always makes me feel like a failure.

* Wishing I could take it all back.

* I want to retreat and hide; it's hard to face her or even speak with her.

* Not having any rational explanation for my behavior leaves me feeling defective.

* I feel lonely and isolated. I just want to stay in bed.

* I have so much shame after behaving so badly.

Maybe you've had a similar experience. Has your reaction to a person or an event been out of proportion? Have you overreacted? We all do this at one time or another! This happens when we aren't bringing awareness to our experiences as they are happening. As you can see from the notes that Cary wrote about her experience, it left her feeling worse *and* it reinforced her negative beliefs.

Try This! Now, can you bring awareness to at least one experience that created an emotional whiteout like the one just described? Were there events that led up to the triggering event, or did it occur out of the blue? What were your thoughts and emotions? How did you react? What were the consequences? How did you feel the next day after the emotional blizzard had passed? Record your experience in your journal.

Reacting quickly to a triggering situation or person is a hard-wired response to help us deal with a threat and the painful emotions that precede it. It works in the short term, but it usually has long-term consequences. Are you able to bring awareness to the short-term benefit (i.e., the release of painful emotions) and long-term consequences of emotionally charged behavior (i.e., hurting others, damaging relationships)?

Avoidance as a Strategy for Dealing with Negative Beliefs

Another strategy for getting rid of painful emotions is to try to avoid experiencing them at all. How you view a problem, a difficulty, or a challenge can be greatly influenced by how you view yourself. You might be quick to blame your flaws or imperfections. You might have thoughts like "If I wasn't lacking in this way, I wouldn't have this problem." You can see how certain challenges or problems are going to trigger your negative beliefs. This can often lead you to avoid situations that might trigger your negative beliefs. Over time, you might find yourself avoiding an entire area of life, because every time you are exposed to it, you feel bad about yourself. Can you think of situations, places, or people you avoid because it tends to make you feel bad about yourself? Use your journal to record your answer.

＊ kelly ＊ When I was younger, I enjoyed playing on my school's volleyball team. It was great to put on my uniform, learn a new sport, get to know the girls on my team, and get spirited and enthusiastic for games. After some time, however, I started to feel like my skill wasn't progressing as much as some of my teammates. We all started as beginners, but some girls were now playing exceptionally well—getting all of their overhand serves over and spiking the ball constantly. I was still figuring out how to do that, and I felt awkward and inferior that I couldn't play as well as they did. So I stayed on the team, but my heart wasn't in it. I would look for excuses not to do certain drills in practice (because I thought I wouldn't be able to do them right). I would elect to sit on the bench for a game, and I would encourage others to take my spot. One day, I twisted my knee in practice, and while it did hurt for several days, I decided to take a few weeks off. This way, I wouldn't have to feel awkward in practice. I could just avoid volleyball, and I didn't even have to admit to everyone else that I didn't want to do it anymore because I felt bad about myself.

In Chapter 2, you identified behaviors that help you cope with feelings of inadequacy, unworthiness, and defectiveness. Let's say you identified avoidance as one of the behaviors that you engage in to make yourself feel better. After that, in Chapter 3 you identified your values—what really matters to you. In doing so, you may have recognized the negative impact that avoidance has on your life—how it prevents you from attaining the life that you want to lead, aligned with your values. In the short term it can feel better to ignore or avoid something that's triggering for you. Whether your version of avoidance consists of not opening an email, ignoring a text, missing a deadline, or avoiding a conversation with someone, the result is the same: you might feel better in the moment, but avoidance usually makes the problem worse, and in turn it makes you feel worse about yourself. So these tactics tend to reinforce your negative beliefs about yourself. We want to change those beliefs. That is why we focus on values and directing your behavior to live in service of your values rather than in service of your fears and negative beliefs.

So far we've been talking about the emotions that are related to your negative beliefs—shame, hurt, sadness, loneliness, anger, and so on. When we experience these emotions, we feel pain. It's a natural urge to take immediate action to get rid of the pain. Over time we figure out that these efforts cause more pain, and we understand that it doesn't work. So what *does* work? The solution is to change the way we relate to our pain.

At the beginning of the chapter we talked about the movie *Inside Out*. In this movie we find out that we can't experience joy without sadness. In fact, all of our emotions, whether we categorize them as good or bad, serve an important function in our lives. And, equally important, we can't eliminate the emotions we don't like. We must experience pain or we won't experience pleasure. When we accept that pain and difficult emotions are part of the human experience, we can stop fighting it. If you aren't fighting it, then you aren't creating more of it.

If you are having trouble accepting this concept, no worries—you are not alone. You might be familiar with the Serenity Prayer:

> God, grant me the serenity to accept the things I cannot change, courage to change the things I can, and wisdom to know the difference.

This simple prayer is used in twelve-step programs for overcoming addictions (which you may or may not be familiar with), and it can also be helpful in bringing more awareness to your struggle and how you can change it. And you don't need to practice any specific religion—or any religion at all—to understand the message.

So, what *can't* we control? We can't control our thoughts, our bodily sensations, our impulses and urges, our emotions, and the behavior of others. What *can* we control? We can control our behavior in response to all of the things we can't control—that is, the choices we make, and the actions we take. Does this make sense? Do you feel more empowered knowing what you have control over in your life?

✴ kelly ✴ This message really resonates with me. It's important for me to differentiate between what I do have control over and what I don't. Sometimes I wish I could control others' actions. The fact that I am not able to control the way that my friends act, especially if it is upsetting me, frustrates me. But I do feel much better when I focus on what I can do. While I may not be able to change my friend's behavior, I can tell her how her behavior makes me feel. It feels much more productive than getting frustrated about what I can't control. For example, one of my roommates (who is a close friend) happens to be incredibly messy. Sometimes I can ignore her clutter and dirty dishes. Other times—particularly when I'm feeling stressed with school—it really bothers me. I get angry, wishing that I could just make her be clean. No matter how much we speak about it, her behavior doesn't really change, though I think it is important that I share how I am feeling with her. Another thing I do to make myself feel better is to focus on my own space. I'll go into my room, get my own space organized, and find some comfort in that.

We receive lots of messages that give us the impression that we can control our internal experiences in the same way we can control tangible objects in our environment (for example, if you hate a shirt, you can throw it out or give it away). We hear messages like "Calm down," "Don't worry," "Don't be sad," "Pull yourself together," "Chill out," and so on. As a child, you probably learned not to touch a hot stove or you would get burned. So you avoided the hot stove so you wouldn't get burned. That's a good thing. It makes sense that an experience like that might lead us to believe that we can get rid of internal pain by avoiding things that cause it. So yes, to some extent you can engage in avoidance, but you might have discovered in Chapter 3 that when you do you end up missing out on parts of your life that are important to you.

The emotion of fear is connected to our negative beliefs about ourselves. So let's look at fear a little more closely. Here's a little thought experiment to help you understand the problem with trying to control your emotions.

Suppose I tell you that in a moment a lion will enter the room, and that this lion preys only on people who show fear or attempt to run away. This lion is incredibly sensitive and will be able to detect the slightest trace of fear that comes up for you. As long as you don't feel afraid and don't try to run away, you'll

115

be completely safe and the lion won't eat you. But if you experience even a trace of fear or try to run, the lion will notice this and eat you.

What would happen? You'd probably start feeling terrified. Can you control that fear? Can you make yourself not feel afraid? How about running? Do you think you could control whether you'd run? Can you make yourself not run? You might be able to stop yourself from running, but could you stop yourself from feeling afraid in the same way?

Now think about what would happen if I told you that as long as you pet the lion, it won't eat you. What would you do? You'd probably start petting it, right? What if I told you that as long as you feed the lion, it won't eat you? What would you do? You'd probably offer it some food. The point here is that controlling our behaviors and what we do with our hands and feet is very different from trying to control our emotional responses. Thoughts, feelings, and sensations aren't like objects in the world. We can't move them around and control them.

Changing and controlling your behavior is very different from attempting to change your internal experiences. We can't relate to our internal experiences the way we do to objects in the world. It just doesn't work. Our thoughts, sensations, emotions, impulses, and memories are in us, and we can't run away or escape from ourselves.

Pain and suffering happen to 100 percent of people. At one point or another, everyone feels disappointed, criticized, lonely, or sad. Have you ever managed to permanently remove an emotion? Have you been able to get a certain thought to never show up in your brain again? It almost seems like the more you don't want those experiences, the more you have them. The more you try to suppress the pain that accompanies your negative beliefs or push it away with reinforcing behaviors, the more intense and painful it becomes. Resisting the emotional pain connected to those beliefs just makes it stronger. For all your efforts at control, it actually makes your negative beliefs stronger.

Try This! Now we'd like you to identify thoughts and feelings that you have tried to avoid. Can you think of instances in which your attempts to avoid these thoughts or feelings have prevented you from doing something that was important to you? Has this gotten in the way of any of your identified values? List these, and describe the ways this has limited your efforts to live a more meaningful life.

Now, on one side of an index card, write the thoughts or feelings that you've tried to get rid of or avoid. On the other side of the same index card, write the areas of your life and values that these avoidance efforts have been keeping you from pursuing and experiencing. Imagine throwing the card away to get rid of those painful thoughts and feelings. Do you recognize what else you are throwing away?

Vanessa's Experience

Vanessa has always been afraid of trying new things. She's very comfortable in her day-to-day routine, and she doesn't like to stray from it. During the week, she goes to school and sports practice, and on Friday nights, she goes to the mall with her two closest friends—they eat at Chipotle and then see a movie. Recently, one of her friends, Serena, has been hanging out with a new group of kids at school. She invited Vanessa and their other friend to go over to her new friend's house to hang out with a bunch of people on Friday night, instead of going to the movies. At first, Vanessa was offended and felt like Serena was picking other friends over her. Vanessa told her friend how she was feeling, and Serena responded by saying that she was really looking forward to introducing her new friends to her old friends, and that this would be a great opportunity for it. Vanessa told Serena that they should just do it a different night, because Friday is Movie Night. Serena didn't understand Vanessa's stubbornness, and ultimately Vanessa spent Friday night at home.

Here is Vanessa's 3x5 card:

What I'm avoiding: *the discomfort I feel meeting new people and trying new things*

My values: *being a good friend and nurturing my friendships*

When Vanessa opted out of Serena's plan she avoided the discomfort, but she also lost out on time with her friend and the opportunity to meet new people and make new friends. Can you see how Vanessa's avoidance pulled her further away from her values?

Emotional pain is what drives us to engage in unhelpful coping behaviors. You hurt, and you don't want to hurt, so you react to eliminate your emotional pain. You already know that these behaviors don't get rid of your pain. In fact, they only increase your pain. You can't get rid of your painful emotions, or your negative thoughts—they will always pop up. So how do you deal with your painful emotions when they surface? You learn some strategies for accepting them. You are probably wondering why you would want to learn to accept them when they cause you pain.

First, let's look at what happens when emotions surface from a situation or an interaction that triggers negative beliefs. You have intense feelings, they are painful, and they probably remind you of other times when you've experienced the pain. Suddenly you are in that emotional whiteout. You can't see anything in the present. You are temporarily blind, and you react in ways that have become automatic but are also unhelpful and self-defeating. Again, when the emotional storm has cleared, you see that your reaction created additional problems. As we've already stated, you can't get rid of your emotions, but you can learn to tolerate and manage them. Let's take a look.

Tolerating and Managing Your Emotions

At times we engage in activities that keep us in the emotional state that is causing us pain. Often we are not even aware of this, because it's become an automatic behavior, and our survival instinct draws us toward these behaviors. There are three things that keep our emotions going:

1. Rumination—you keep thinking about the same painful experience over and over again.

2. Avoidance—you don't face or accept the emotion for what it is.

3. Emotion-driven behavior—you engage in behaviors that are self-defeating and hurt yourself and/or others.

Try This! Can you identify with any of the behaviors that keep your painful emotions going? Record them in your journal.

Let's take a look at what Kennedy wrote:

When I was younger, I got in a car accident; I wasn't badly injured or anything, but it was very scary, and I frequently have nightmares about it. That's why I don't like riding in cars. Luckily, we live in a small town, and it's easy for me to walk to and from school. But sometimes it's not possible for me to walk to the places I need to get to. These situations make me so afraid. I just keep thinking about the accident. I can't keep myself from playing it over and over in my head. Continually avoiding situations that trigger my fear has limited my life and my relationships. And it makes me feel worse about myself, and less confident in my ability to make new friends and try new things.

The key to dealing with difficult emotions is to choose an action or a behavior that won't make you feel worse about yourself or make the situation or relationship worse. *Distress tolerance* is a skill that can help you make a choice that doesn't create additional consequences. (You may have heard of cognitive behavioral therapy, or CBT; distress tolerance is a skill learned in a specific type of CBT called dialectical behavioral therapy, or DBT, developed by psychologist Marsha Linehan.) The primary goal is to get you through your emotional whiteout without making the situation worse. We've talked about this in previous chapters, but it's important to restate the fact that all thoughts, emotions, and bodily sensations are temporary—they pass with time. They are not permanent. It is important to remember this fact when you are experiencing difficult emotions and you feel a compelling urge to get rid of them quickly. As you probably already know, this tends to cause more problems, even if it seems effective in the short term.

Bringing awareness to how you've coped with painful emotions and situations will help you make better choices in the future. The emotions that you experience when your negative beliefs about yourself get triggered often feel overwhelming and intolerable. Of course, your natural impulse is to get rid of them as fast as possible. Let's look at the ways in which your reactions are causing more problems. (This is adapted from *The Dialectical Behavior Therapy Skills Workbook* by McKay et al., 2007.)

The following are behaviors we tend to engage in when we are reacting to painful emotions, along with the costs associated with engaging in those behaviors. As you identify the ones that are relevant for you, avoid judging yourself; practice self-compassion, and remember that your reactions made sense in the short term.

Behaviors: Blaming, criticizing, challenging, or being resistant toward others

Costs: Loss of friendship, romantic relationships, and family; people avoid you; you hurt the feelings of others

Behaviors: You appear to be compliant, but you rebel by procrastinating, complaining, being tardy, or performing poorly

Costs: Put up with unhealthy relationships; cause problems at school, work, or home

Behaviors: Controlling others as a way to get what you want

Costs: You alienate people and cause them pain

Behaviors: Trying to impress others and get attention

Costs: You miss out on real connections with people and alienate them

Behaviors: Using manipulation, exploitation or temptation

Costs: You ruin relationships, create a climate of distrust, and alienate people

Behaviors: Isolation, social withdrawal, disconnecting and withdrawing from others

Costs: You miss out on potentially enjoyable experiences and good things; you feel depressed, alone, and lonely

Behaviors: Excessive autonomy, appearing independent and self-reliant or engaging in solitary activities such as reading, watching TV, or computer use

Costs: You spend more time by yourself and feel more depressed, disconnected, and alone

Behaviors: Seeking excitement or distraction through any compulsive behavior, risk taking, or physical activity

Costs: You develop health problems, relationship problems, and experience feelings of shame

Behaviors: Seeking excitement through drugs, alcohol, and food

Costs: You develop dependencies and addiction and suffer relationship problems and health consequences

Behaviors: Escaping through dissociation, denial, fantasy, or other internal forms of withdrawal

Costs: You struggle with feelings of loneliness, shame, and depression

Behaviors: Relying too much on others, giving in, not being independent, behaving passively, avoiding conflict, trying to please others

Costs: You overburden relationships with your needs, yet you don't get your needs met

In your journal, list any additional behaviors and their costs.

Try This!   Use your journal to record the behaviors that you engage in to cope with negative emotions and their associated costs.

Remember Cary from earlier? She and her friend, Antonia, had a negative interaction. Here's what Cary wrote:

I was blaming and criticizing toward Antonia and I was relying too much on her. It compromised our friendship and overburdened her and our relationship.

Cary was able to recognize the behavior she had engaged in and its costs, or consequences. In recognizing the costs of negative behavior, Cary can be more intentional about the way that she acts when dealing with difficult emotions.

Pain versus Suffering

We've already talked about the reality of pain. It is part of the human experience, and there is no avoiding it. With the previous exercise you brought awareness to the consequences associated with behaviors that we think are going to eliminate our pain, or that might provide us with a break from the pain. But these behaviors cause more pain—let's call this additional pain or suffering. We can eliminate this additional suffering from our lives. Doesn't that sound great? We will inevitably experience pain—that's not an option—but we don't have to experience the additional suffering—that *is* an option. We usually opt in to that suffering unknowingly by behaving in ways that create additional pain and suffering. When we try to eliminate the pain and suffering that is part of living we tend to behave in ways that create more pain and suffering.

So now that you know you can opt out of the additional suffering, you need some tools for dealing with your pain in a new way. You need to replace your unhelpful behaviors with healthy or helpful behaviors. You need some behaviors that will help you tolerate the whiteout period—when you are so overwhelmed with emotion that you can't make a rational, helpful choice.

Distracting Activities

Distracting activities are useful because they keep you occupied until the emotional storm has cleared and you have some

125

distance from the triggering event, situation, or person. They are not about trying to avoid or escape your emotions; they are just about getting you to a place where you can make a clear evaluation. Distracting activities are a safety measure that will prevent you from engaging in behaviors that are unhealthy or unhelpful. Earlier we talked about the multi-car pileup accidents that we see on the news when there's a blizzard. Most often this is the result of people who continue to drive when their view from the car or the general visibility is impaired or limited. They could avoid the pileup if they stopped driving as soon as they recognized that the conditions made driving unhelpful and potentially harmful. Distracting activities are a way to minimize or avoid any additional problems (additional suffering).

✳ kelly ✳ When I feel an emotional storm coming on, I try my best to get physical and mental distance from it. It's definitely easier said than done, but something that's worked for me is to first physically remove myself from whatever it is that is making me upset. If it's an event or another person, I'll politely excuse myself and go somewhere that will allow me to calm down. Now that I've physically removed myself from the situation, I have the mental distance, too.

Here are some ideas for pleasurable activities. Use them as inspiration, and experiment with what works best for you.

Physical activities, in addition to being a distraction, provide endorphins, which are a natural pain reliever and an antidepressant. This partial list is meant to inspire you. Check, circle, or otherwise mark the activities that appeal to you:

running	boating
swimming	water polo
jogging	basketball
walking	Pilates
backpacking	kite surfing
hiking	bowling
team sports	yoga
windsurfing	snow skiing
biking	boxing
golf	weight lifting
volleyball	fishing
ballet	TRX
spin class	water aerobics
tennis	rowing
Zumba	aerobic classes

CrossFit

farming or gardening

kickboxing

kickball

frisbee

lacrosse

handball

stretching

racquetball

paddle boating

horseback riding

ice skating

water volleyball

rock climbing

martial arts

rollerblading

jumping rope

roller skating

kayaking

rugby

water skiing

shuffleboard

scuba diving

sailing

snorkeling

snowmobiling

walking your dog

snowshoeing

soccer

speed skating

softball

trampoline

surfing

wrestling

Are there other physical activities that would be helpful for you? Write them on the page, or in your journal.

Here is a partial list of other activities for inspiration. Check, circle, or otherwise mark the activities that appeal to you:

reading	church activities
family time	beach
going to a movie	eating out
computer games	playing
puzzles	music
drawing	housework
renting movies	scrapbooking
listening to music	crafts
entertaining friends	journaling
shopping	watching sports
traveling	photography
sleeping/napping	playing cards
socializing	cooking/baking
sewing	working on cars
ping pong	writing
knitting	animal care
pool	painting

Are there other hobbies that you enjoy that would help you deal with your pain? Write them here, or in your journal.

When you are struggling, it's easy to get caught up in your own experience and forget that there are other people who are struggling as well. Studies show that we feel better when we get outside of ourselves and focus our attention on helping others. To that end, here are some suggestions for volunteering. Check, circle, or otherwise mark the volunteer activities that appeal to you:

environmental organizations

food banks

blood banks

after-school programs

disaster relief

parks and outdoor areas

museums

tutoring programs

boy and girls clubs

mentoring programs

literacy programs

hospitals

SPCA or animal programs

nursing homes

retirement communities

homeless shelters

libraries

political organizations

aquariums

Habitat for Humanity

community cleanup projects

community gardens

volunteer coaching

writing to a military person

Special Olympics

Big Brother or Big Sister

volunteering in daycare centers

American Red Cross

Try This! Identify the distracting activities in each area (physical activities, other activities, and volunteer activities) that you want to start with. You can always add other activities later or remove activities that you find you don't enjoy or that provided limited distraction. Write them in your journal. Also, you might want to put them in the notes section of your smartphone so you can access them when you aren't home. As you try them out, keep track of the ones that you find most successful.

Time is a consideration when choosing a distracting activity. Identify activities that will be helpful when you have more time as well as activities that will be effective for you when you are short on time.

✳ kelly ✳ Here are the distraction activities I turn to: take ten deep breaths, go outside and get some fresh air, call my parents, call a friend, clean my space, listen to a podcast, read a book, exercise (if I don't have a lot of time, I do just a short activity that will get my heart rate up, like jumping jacks), drink a glass of cold water.

Pleasant Memories

When we're feeling bad and experiencing painful emotions, we often lose sight of the good things that we've experienced. Accessing these memories can remind us that this bad period is temporary. In *The Bullying Workbook for Teens* (Lohmann and Taylor, 2013), the authors suggest making a Code Blue box—a box containing things that remind you of happy, pleasant, and fun times. You can add favorite objects, mementos, photos, and cards and letters that remind you of those times. It's not practical to have a box when you're not at home, so we have some alternative suggestions. You can take photos of the objects that remind you of more pleasant times and create a photo album on your smartphone so you can access it any time you need a boost. You can have someone you love record a voice memo on your phone that you can listen to when you need to be reminded that you're not alone. And you can create an area in your space (bedroom or dorm) where you have photos of the people you love.

✱ **kelly** ✱ My "Code Blue box" is a mini-collection of letters and cards from my friends and family that I can read through to remind myself of how loved and supported I am. As I sit in my room writing, I am looking at my stack of cards—the ones at the top are from my most recent birthday. It makes me smile, even when my "here-and-now" is maybe unhappy. Back home, I've created a bulletin board on the back of my door with photos, (more) cards, and other memorabilia like concert and sports game tickets to remind me of all the wonderful times I've had in my life. It gives me hope for the wonderful times that are ahead of me!

Putting It All Together

In this chapter, you learned more about your emotions as well as why you need the ones you don't like, and how to accept them. When negative beliefs get triggered, we get flooded with painful emotions that can feel overwhelming and intolerable. Our reaction to this pain can create suffering that is avoidable if we bring awareness to our experience and remember to engage in activities that can provide the time we need to get through the emotional whiteout. Once we can evaluate the situation more clearly, we can make choices that keep us moving in the direction of our values. Now you have a better understanding of your negative beliefs as well as your relationship with your thoughts and emotions. In the next chapter, we are going to look more closely at behavioral reactions and communication skills.

chapter 7

Helpful Behaviors and Communication

In Chapter 2 you brought awareness to the traps and triggers associated with your beliefs about yourself and others. If you are in situations that trigger your feelings of inadequacy, unworthiness, defectiveness, or failure, your behaviors are likely an expression of your thoughts and emotions. This is particularly true when you haven't made the connection that you are acting on urges in an effort to get rid of feeling bad about yourself.

Your automatic coping behaviors may provide some temporary relief from the negative thoughts, uncomfortable emotions, and sensations. But it's likely that you feel as bad or worse after the temporary relief subsides. As we've said, your behaviors are designed to protect you, but they are tied more closely to your survival instinct that, when triggered, has you reacting in a fight, flight, or freeze mode. This reaction served a very useful purpose for our ancestors, who were frequently challenged by life-threatening situations, but for most of us it is no longer useful. Modern humans still face some threats that require an immediate, potentially life-saving reaction, like jumping out of the way of an oncoming car, but it's more likely that the triggering situations you face only *feel* life threatening.

When you are in a situation that makes you feel that a part of yourself you view as flawed or inadequate is going to be exposed, it makes sense that you would react as if your life were in danger. In this chapter we are going to help you understand your reaction more deeply, link your behaviors to the values you identified in Chapter 3, and shift your perspective to enable you to become more flexible in reaction to triggering events. Ultimately, we want to help you bring awareness to the helpful behavioral responses that are connected to your values. This shift in behavior won't eliminate the pain that comes with being an imperfect person in an imperfect world, but it will prevent the additional suffering that you experience when you react with unhelpful behaviors.

* **kelly** * When I'm feeling stressed or overwhelmed about a big to-do task, whether it's a big school assignment or a tough conversation with a friend, I'll often make excuses to myself about why I should wait to do it, why I need to get other things done first, and so on. This is mostly because I am intimidated. In response, I find myself spending time on less time-sensitive projects—time I should be spending on that assignment.

I'll start getting ahead on my history reading, or decide it's the perfect time to print out pictures from last summer's family vacation to add them to my photo wall. I know that I'm avoiding what I really have to do, but I do it anyway because it distracts me from what's weighing on me. Also, didn't I have to do these things at some point? This is totally productive, right? Eh ... ultimately, this behavior backfires. I end up working on the big assignment at the last minute. Because I didn't give myself as much time as I should've, I feel incredibly frustrated because I know it's not as good as it could be.

Can you see how the unhelpful reaction to a situation ends up making you feel worse in the long term because it reinforces your feelings of inadequacy, unworthiness, defectiveness, imperfection, or failure?

Try This! Identify recurring triggering situations, along with their associated thoughts or beliefs, emotions, and sensations, and your behavioral reaction. Now fill in the consequences that you experience in the aftermath of acting on your behavioral urge.

When you bring awareness to the consequences, can you see how these behaviors result in more pain by reinforcing your beliefs about yourself?

Can you imagine allowing enough time between the triggering situation and acting on your urge to make a different choice?

✳ kelly ✳ Here's what I wrote, based on the experience I described.

Triggering situation: *A big school assignment*

Thoughts or beliefs: *It's going to be too hard, I'm not smart enough for this, I won't do as well as I want to*

Emotions: *Preoccupied, stressed*

Bodily sensations: *Feeling sick to my stomach, restless or having difficulty falling asleep at night*

Behavioral reaction or urge: *Ignore the big assignment and distract myself by focusing on something else*

Consequences: *I end up more stressed, I don't do as well as I wanted to—just as I worried initially*

We want to reinforce an important fact: you have alternatives. You can make a different choice. You don't need to default to your survival mode.

While this shift might sound simple, it's certainly not easy. The survival behavioral reaction is automatic and often outside of your awareness—meaning that you don't have to give any thought to it. It's easy because you're on autopilot. Choosing the value-based behavioral response takes awareness and mindfulness (as we discussed in Chapter 5)—focusing on the present moment. This is the opposite of autopilot. However, with time, your value-driven behavior will become more automatic. But before that can happen, you need to identify very specific helpful behavioral responses.

Try This! Take that triggering situation and the behavioral reaction from the preceding exercise. Now think about what your value-driven behavioral response in that situation would be. What are the potential benefits associated with that choice?

Now, can you imagine how you might feel differently about yourself if you shifted from your current automatic behavior to your value-driven behavior?

Can you compare and contrast the feelings about yourself and the reactions from others when you engage in your automatic behavioral reaction versus your value-driven response?

✷ **kelly** ✷ Here's what I wrote.

Triggering situation: *A big school assignment*

Automatic behavioral reaction: *Ignore the big assignment and distract myself by focusing on something else*

Value-driven behavioral response: *Bringing attention to the big assignment, working on it*

The potential benefits: *Doing well, decreasing unnecessary stress*

Try This! Now compare and contrast how the different actions (automatic behavioral reaction versus value-driven response) in your triggering situation make you and others feel.

> **✻ kelly ✻** Here is how I completed this exercise:
>
> **Automatic behavioral reaction:** Ignore the big assignment and distract myself by focusing on something else
>
> **Feelings about myself:** *I am not smart enough for this*
>
> **Reactions from others:** *She must not care about this very much*
>
> **Value-driven behavioral response:** Bringing attention to the big assignment, working on it
>
> **Feelings about myself:** *I am successful*
>
> **Reactions from others:** *She is hardworking*

Are you beginning to see the upside of making a new choice?

Another important aspect of making a helpful choice is choosing to communicate in a way that builds and strengthens your relationships with others. Let's look more closely at communication.

What Is Your Communication Saying about You?

When you've reacted to your negative beliefs, it's likely that your communication style has been a bit off—maybe too harsh, or too timid, or unclear and ineffective. You may have difficulty expressing your feelings, or you may express them angrily in the heat of the moment. You may easily misinterpret what others are saying because you are viewing them through the filter of your negative beliefs, particularly during a triggering experience.

We've talked about thoughts and the need to change our relationship to thoughts. Now, you know that when we attach to our thoughts they tend to confirm or reinforce our negative beliefs. The same is true for the statements that come from other people. It's easy for us to attach to key words or statements and filter them through the lens of our negative beliefs. This usually prevents us from hearing the whole message, because we have attached to the part of the message that is confirming our negative beliefs and our predictions based on our negative beliefs.

In order to become a better listener, you must observe without evaluating or judging. When you get triggered, you are flooded with negative thoughts and emotions—you're in the whiteout. You will likely latch on to comments that confirm your negative beliefs about yourself and your expectations of others. When this happens, there is no flexibility in your thinking—you default to the fixed (automatic) thoughts and behaviors that reinforce your negative beliefs. You might jump to conclusions without taking a closer look at the situation. You might unknowingly present to others as critical, inflexible, judgmental, and defensive. Bringing awareness to your experience (as you did in Chapter 2) and taking on the role of an investigative journalist can help you make the shift from unhelpful communication to helpful communication. This means that you are curious and you want to find out more before you reach a conclusion or provide a response.

Many of the negative beliefs about yourself have been operating outside of your awareness, driving your behaviors and communication in ways that you haven't fully realized. When you get triggered and you have a strong urge to react, bring awareness to that strong urge and use it as an indication that you need to slow down and examine your current situation.

Confirmatory bias can be a major obstacle to healthy communication. This is the tendency to see only what supports your beliefs and your story. When your negative beliefs get triggered, your mind takes a shortcut and predicts the outcome based on past experience; there isn't any room for information that would disconfirm your negative belief. This is a protective measure—we have a negativity bias that protects us from harm—but as you probably already know, it can cause some problems. This can be especially true when it comes to listening to others.

Listening Skills

Being a good listener is essential for healthy communication and important for building meaningful and lasting relationships. Before we introduce the active listening skills, let's look at the blocks to active listening.

Listening Blocks

It's no secret that there are constant distractions in our daily lives that can prevent us from being better communicators. In the best of situations, it's challenging to be a good listener when we have so many distractions, but add in the negative beliefs that get triggered, and it can feel impossible. We all use listening blocks, whether we are aware of it or not. It's habitual behavior that gets in the way of connecting more deeply with others.

Types of Listening Blocks

Now, let's bring some awareness to some of the listening blocks that can get in the way of our communication with others. Below is a list of some primary listening blocks that we tend to engage in, particularly when our negative beliefs get triggered. When we aren't fully present during a triggering experience, it creates obstacles to understanding what the other person is trying to communicate and limits our ability to communicate effectively. These blocks are almost always automatic reactions to triggering experiences. Identify which ones are relevant for you.

Comparing You're not listening because your focus is on comparing yourself to the other person and/or the situation.

Mind reading You're focused on figuring out the other person's "real" thoughts and feelings rather than fully listening. This is especially common when your negative belief is triggered, because you're trying to predict the outcome based on your past experiences.

Rehearsing You're busy rehearsing what you're going to say instead of listening fully.

Filtering You'll let your mind wander or may stop listening when you hear a particular tone or subject that you find unpleasant or triggering.

Judging You stop listening to the message and instead try to judge what the other person might do. This is especially common during a triggering conversation.

Sparring You are quick to disagree or debate.

Being right Your primary goal is to not be seen as wrong.

Derailing You change the subject to derail the conversation. This may be one of your "go to" tactics to avoid revealing parts of yourself that might expose your flaws.

Placating You are so focused on coming across as kind and supportive (oftentimes to avoid criticism) that you're not really listening.

Try This! The first step in overcoming your listening blocks is to identify them and link them to domains, people, and situations. Write in your journal, being as specific and detailed as possible.

✳ **kelly** ✳ In the family domain, I struggle with the "mind reading" listening block. Because I know everyone in my immediate family so well, I often assume that I already know what they're going to say before they say it, particularly during an argument. Like, "Yes, Mom, I know that you want me to make my bed and finally do some of my laundry." This behavior connects to the idea that I worry that my mom will criticize me, even before I know what she wants to talk about. Often, this will result in the other family member feeling frustrated, which actually makes for a worse interaction than if I had listened with openness.

Can you see how your negative beliefs can get in the way of healthy communication—in particular, truly listening to the other person? If we don't bring awareness to our blocks, we are stuck in a pattern of communication that is likely to reinforce our negative beliefs.

Expressing Yourself

Another key aspect of communication is expressing your-self. Maybe you haven't learned how to express your needs in an effective way, or maybe you figured out that you were more likely to get attention by acting out, or maybe you have given up on the idea of having your needs met. If you feel flawed, not worthy, or not good enough, it's likely that at some point you concluded that you don't deserve to have your needs met. You may worry that others might criticize or make fun of you for your needs, or that the needs of others take priority.

Identifying your needs and your feelings can be difficult. And they can scare us, because they can make us feel vulner-able, and they can bring disappointment, sadness, loneliness, depression, anger, and longing. Hiding parts of yourself from others and protecting yourself can be a distraction from identi-fying your needs. Bringing your needs to awareness can trigger uncomfortable feelings.

And when you get triggered, the negative emotion can be so overwhelming that you may have a difficult time identifying your feelings and needs. In other words, you may get angry and lash out, but once the emotional whiteout has passed you realize that you were actually feeling sad. Sadness feels more vulnerable than anger. Remember Cary from the previous chapter? She was missing Antonia, but rather than stating her need to spend more time with Antonia, she lashed out at her. After the emotional whiteout, she was able to identify her true feelings and needs.

Try This! Spend some time reviewing the exercises that you've completed. Can you identify needs that you haven't expressed? Can you bring awareness to the way in which hiding parts of yourself that you view as flawed also results in hiding your needs from others? Can you identify times when it might be more difficult for you to express your needs? Write about this in your journal.

* **kelly** * It's something I'm definitely working on, but I continue to find it challenging to express my needs all of the time. For example, sometimes at school I'd like some alone time to relax and take a breather between classes, club meetings, and social time with friends. (Sometimes I need it more than others!) It can be challenging to explain to a friend who might want to hang out with me or do something with me at school that I need time to myself. When I ignore this need, I'm often less fun to be around and end up feeling a lot more tired than I did to begin with.

Try This! When you're dealing with negative beliefs, you are constantly bombarded with negative thoughts that your mind generates outside of your control. You've learned the importance of mindfulness for creating distance from these thoughts, and not attaching to them. But what happens when the critical comments are coming from others? How do you receive their criticism? How do you handle it? And how do you respond?

✳ kelly ✳ When I was younger, I had a really difficult time dealing with criticism. I didn't think about the fact that criticism can come from a good place; I just assumed that when someone shares criticism with you, it's because they are upset with you or don't like some aspect of who you are. Now I know that's not true, and I work to be more open to criticism, particularly from people who care about me and are looking out for my best interest.

Try This! Take a moment to write down your habitual, instinctive responses when you experience a communication as criticism. Do you counterattack with criticism, become defensive, placate, change the subject, withdraw, shut down, criticize yourself, or immediately apologize so you don't have to hear more? Explore your responses in each of your domains.

It's likely that you have spent a decent amount of time reacting to real and perceived criticism from others and this has prevented you from identifying your needs and learning how to express them. Maybe you've tried expressing your needs before, and you were left feeling like your needs don't matter as much as, or are less important than, the needs of others. This may be an experience that you have with people in general or it may tend to happen with specific individuals or types of individuals. In the past, your requests may have been met with disapproval or judgment.

Maybe you've never practiced expressing your needs. You may feel like you need to make a case for why the other person should fulfill your request. And it's likely that you have been denying your own needs in order to please others, gain approval, or avoid disappointing others and suffering the consequences. You might feel that in relationships your needs don't get met and you spend most of your time meeting the needs of others.

Try This! Think of a recent situation in which a need of yours went unexpressed or you felt like you misfired with your request. Write down the details you remember.

Can you see why it's important to recognize your need in the moment and express it when it is appropriate? When negative beliefs are triggered, we are not in the moment, and we can find ourselves asking for things that relate to past experiences or fears about the future. In terms of expressing our needs, this often means we make requests that aren't actually in line with the current situation. The requests are tangled up with a need from the past that was never expressed. Oftentimes, when it is finally expressed, it is delivered with negative emotions that seem out of line with the current situation. This is understandable and happens to everyone. It's important to practice self-compassion when you recognize that you have these unexpressed needs from the past that are still affecting you in the present.

Active Listening

Our negative beliefs sensitize us to messages that might indicate something is wrong with us. We likely misunderstand communications or assume that the other person was saying something negative about us, and we don't ask for clarification. This can happen in person, and it almost always happens over text, because these are short communications, and you can't see the other person's body language or hear the tone of her voice. It really is a setup for miscommunication. Active listening can help eliminate these misunderstandings. It is best to use these three steps over the telephone or in person.

Step 1: Paraphrasing

Paraphrasing is using your own words to state what the other person has said. It is especially important that you paraphrase when you're having a conversation about something that's triggering your negative beliefs. This will stop miscommunication in the moment. It makes for clear communication by eliminating misunderstandings that might be distorted by your negative beliefs about yourself.

Example: "If I heard you correctly, you're saying that ... "

Step 2: Clarifying

Clarifying is an extension of paraphrasing that involves asking questions until you have a clear understanding of what's being communicated to you. This step allows you to get more information to fill in the details about what is being said to you, or it may help you understand more about someone's mood. When we have a negative belief, if someone is expressing upset we might assume that we did something wrong.

Example: "You seem upset. Is it something I did?"

Step 3: Feedback

The final step is to take the information that you've acquired from your conversation and talk about your reaction in a non-judgmental way. This is an opportunity to share your thoughts and feelings. Your experience might be that you understood the message that was communicated to you but you are unclear about how the person is feeling. This is an opportunity to connect more deeply with the other person.

Example: "I understand what you're saying, but can you tell me more about how you are feeling?"

Giving feedback is helpful to the other person too because he can better understand the effectiveness of his communication and quickly correct any misperceptions or miscommunications. It's important that you provide feedback at the time of the conversation and that you are honest (with kindness and compassion) and supportive.

Putting It All Together

Engaging in helpful behavior, including healthy communication, can be challenging. Understanding the benefits of behavior and communication that are aligned with your values is a great source of motivation. When you listen to others and express yourself without the blocks associated with your negative beliefs, you will connect more deeply with everyone. These connections will enhance your life and the lives of others and get you that much closer to understanding and believing that you are fine just as you are!

chapter 8

How Do I Keep Myself on Track?

Now that you've nearly done reading *Just As You Are*, we hope that you're better able to identify the negative beliefs that you have about yourself, how they impact your behavior, and what you can do to eliminate these beliefs to lead a happy, more values-driven life. Now doesn't that sound easy? Well, of course, it isn't. As we mentioned previously, everyone struggles. Everyone also struggles with working to overcome their struggle.

We hope that if you find yourself needing support in this effort, you'll return to this final chapter, which can serve as a *SparkNotes* version of the book. Here you can reference any specific chapter, its theme, and key exercises to refresh your memory on the tools we've outlined in the book and keep you on track with your goals.

Chapter Overviews

In Chapter 1, "What's Up with the Way I Feel about Myself?" we brought awareness to the beliefs that you have about yourself and how they were formed. Think about the stories that various teens shared in the beginning about parts of themselves that they felt they needed to hide. What part (or parts) of yourself did you feel you needed to hide when you wrote your story? Is that still relevant to you now? In what domain—what area of your life—does this feel particularly relevant?

We don't want you to attach to your story, but it's necessary for you to continue to bring awareness to the beliefs about yourself that prevent you from being fully authentic and fully connecting with others. Ideally, we want you to keep track of the domains that are negatively impacted by your beliefs. You will use this information to assist you in making the connection between your beliefs and the actions that result from your beliefs. If you are successful in not acting on your beliefs, then you can identify the urge that you experience (that is, the automatic behavior that you've acted on in the past).

In Chapter 2, "Why Do I Do the Things That I Do?" we explained how negative thoughts and emotions can result from a particular triggering situation and in turn will lead to negative behavior. You identified triggering events, people, and situations that you experience. In the face of this experience, you often engage in behavior that makes you feel better in the short term, but in the long term is damaging and unhelpful. These behaviors that are meant to make you feel better about yourself may make you feel worse about yourself in the end. It's important to remember that you have the power to choose how you react. Need a kick-starter? Look back at the section titled "Triggering Behaviors and Experiences." There we list behaviors and experiences that you may identify with. Read through these again; more may come to mind for you. As we've said, bringing awareness to your behaviors and experiences is the first step toward making different choices that will increase your feelings of self-worth and get you closer to the life that you want. We love to use a technique called a decision tree. Write down a triggering event or situation and draw two arrows—one for the automatic behavior that you have engaged in previously, and one for the behavior that will bring you closer to your values. Draw another arrow from each behavior and add the consequences of each of those behaviors. When you see this on paper, it brings a new awareness to the power of your choices.

In Chapter 3, "Figuring Out What Matters to You," we discussed values, and how living your life based on your values will help you change unhelpful behavior. When you act with your values in mind, you behave in ways that will make you feel better about yourself. These are your valued intentions. Acting on your values isn't easy, so first and foremost it's important that you keep in mind what your values actually are. We suggest that you keep a list of your values and your valued intentions. This list will remind you of what it is that you truly care about, and how you can prioritize what you care about in your day-to-day life. At the beginning of each week, we suggest that you bring awareness to your values as they relate to the areas that you are finding particularly challenging. At the end of each week, you can review your list and see how you did. Remember, you are aiming for progress, not perfection!

In Chapter 4, "Connect to Yourself and Others," we explained the importance of self-compassion. As we've said before, self-compassion will increase your feelings of self-worth, and that sense of self-worth will remain much more stable over time because you are being kind to yourself and judging yourself fairly. If you're feeling stuck about maintaining self-compassion, try this: return to your loving-kindness meditation that is specific to you and your struggles. If a difficult aspect of yourself is your fear of failure, your accompanying aspirational phrase might be "May I be free from fear." Do this regularly, and kick your inner critic to the curb.

In Chapter 5, "Mindfulness and the Monkey Mind," we talked about mindfulness and thought patterns. Mindfulness is a wonderful tool to help you achieve self-acceptance. With the practice of mindfulness, you will avoid getting stuck in thoughts of regret about the past or fearful, worrying thoughts about the future. Without those distractions, you can bring more awareness to what you are grateful for in your life. Want some help getting into the mindful zone? Turn back to Chapter 5 and find our Mindfulness Focusing exercise. This exercise is a step toward observing your current situation for what it is—without your negative beliefs distorting it. This will allow you to give your thoughts and feelings their moment and see them for what they are—temporary experiences that don't require a behavioral reaction. Alternatively, you can find an audio recording on kellyskeen.com.

In Chapter 6, "Emotions and the 'I' of the Storm," you learned more about your emotions, as well as why we need even the ones we don't like and how to accept them (remember the movie *Inside Out*?). You learned about the importance of experiencing your emotions in order to get through difficult periods. If you're experiencing an emotional whiteout, or need help managing your emotions, take another look at the section on distracting activities. There are several lists of suggestions to help you take a break from your difficult emotional situation and find some clarity. We suggest that you take a look at the week ahead of you and identify any situations or events that might trigger uncomfortable emotions for you. For each of those situations or events, choose a distracting activity that will help you weather the emotional storm. It's always helpful to be prepared.

Finally, in Chapter 7, "Helpful Behaviors and Communication," we brought awareness to unhelpful behavioral patterns and provided you with the tools to respond to triggering situations by connecting with your values. This chapter stresses the importance of communication—a crucial piece of this puzzle. How can we make choices to behave in ways that will make our lives better? We need to make decisions that are value-driven. Need help? Look back at the exercise that compares a behavioral reaction and a value-driven response. This will help you recognize how helpful it is to make the choice to change your actions!

Additionally, take a look at the communication skills that we discuss in Chapter 7. We are all challenged in our communication with others, particularly when we are experiencing a triggering situation. What are the skills that you need to work on? We have found that people tend to stop listening as soon as they get triggered, so you might want to start with a focus on listening to others, clarifying so that you are understanding the whole message and not just the part of the message that might be confirming your negative beliefs about yourself.

Putting It All Together—For the Last Time

Above all, it's important to remember that your journey toward self-acceptance—recognizing that you are good, that you are enough, just as you are—requires a lot of effort. You will not accomplish it just from reading this book once, putting it on your shelf, and moving on. However, if you are committed to living a full, values-driven life, then you can achieve it. And remember—you are not alone!

References

Lohmann, R., and J. Taylor. 2013. *The Bullying Workbook for Teens.* Oakland, CA: New Harbinger.

McKay, M., M. Skeen, P. Fanning, and K. Skeen. 2016. *Communication Skills for Teens.* Oakland, CA: New Harbinger.

McKay, M., J. Wood, and J. Brantley. 2007. *The Dialectical Behavior Therapy Skills Workbook.* Oakland, CA: New Harbinger.

Paterson, R. 2016. *How to Be Miserable.* Oakland, CA: New Harbinger.

Salzberg, S. 2002. *Loving-Kindness: The Revolutionary Art of Happiness.* Boulder, CO: Shambhala.

Michelle Skeen, PsyD, has a doctorate in clinical psychology. She is author of seven books, all designed to enhance relationships by emphasizing the importance of identifying core values and valued intentions, limited thinking, mindfulness, self-compassion, empathy, and effective communication and conflict resolution skills. Her passion is coaching individuals in creating and maintaining healthy relationships by bringing awareness to obstacles (fears and beliefs), which often work unconsciously to limit connections with others. Michelle believes that an early introduction and education in core values and healthy communication are essential life skills for success. To that end, Michelle and her daughter, Kelly, coauthored *Communication Skills for Teens* and *Just As You Are*.

Skeen completed her postdoctoral work at the University of California, San Francisco. She codeveloped an empirically validated protocol for the treatment of interpersonal problems that resulted in two books: *Acceptance and Commitment Therapy for Interpersonal Problems* and *The Interpersonal Problems Workbook*. Michelle's work has appeared in more than thirty publications around the world. She hosts a weekly radio show called *Relationships 2.0 with Dr. Michelle Skeen* that airs nationally. To find out more, visit her website at www.michelleskeen.com.

Kelly Skeen is a recent graduate of Georgetown University in Washington, DC. As an American studies major, she concentrated in art and museum studies, and plans to pursue a career expanding access to the visual arts. She is also coauthor of *Communication Skills for Teens* with her mother, Michelle Skeen. Skeen strives every day for greater self-acceptance and to embrace who she really is! To learn more, visit her website at www.kellyskeen.com.

More ⏱Instant Help Books for Teens

An Imprint of New Harbinger Publications

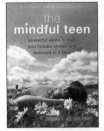

THINK CONFIDENT, BE CONFIDENT FOR TEENS
A Cognitive Therapy Guide to Overcoming Self-Doubt & Creating Unshakable Self-Esteem
ISBN: 978-1608821136 / US $16.95

GET OUT OF YOUR MIND & INTO YOUR LIFE FOR TEENS
A Guide to Living an Extraordinary Life
978-1608821938 / US $15.95

THE MINDFUL TEEN
Powerful Skills to Help You Handle Stress One Moment at a Time
978-1626250802 / US $17.95

STUFF THAT SUCKS
A Teen's Guide to Accepting What You Can't Change & Committing to What You Can
978-1626258655 / US $12.95

THE TEEN GIRL'S SURVIVAL GUIDE
Ten Tips for Making Friends, Avoiding Drama & Coping with Social Stress
ISBN: 978-1626253063 / US $16.95

THE BODY IMAGE WORKBOOK FOR TEENS
Activities to Help Girls Develop a Healthy Body Image in an Image-Obsessed World
978-1626250185 / US $16.95

newharbingerpublications
1-800-748-6273 / newharbinger.com

(VISA, MC, AMEX / prices subject to change without notice)

Follow Us 📘 🐦 📷 📌

Don't miss out on new books in the subjects that interest you.
Sign up for our Book Alerts at **newharbinger.com/bookalerts** 🖱